I0012723

DYLAN FOX

Full Stack Development With Spring Boot 3 And React

Copyright © 2024 by Dylan Fox

All rights reserved. No part of this publication may be reproduced, stored or transmitted in any form or by any means, electronic, mechanical, photocopying, recording, scanning, or otherwise without written permission from the publisher. It is illegal to copy this book, post it to a website, or distribute it by any other means without permission.

First edition

This book was professionally typeset on Reedsy.
Find out more at reedsy.com

Contents

Chapter 1: Introduction to Full Stack Development

I n the realm of software engineering, **full stack development** refers to the development of both the frontend (client side) and backend (server side) parts of an application. A **full stack developer** is capable of working on both sides of the development process, bridging the gap between how users interact with an application (frontend) and how the system processes those interactions (backend). In essence, full stack development covers everything needed to build a fully functional web or mobile application from start to finish.

Frontend Development

Frontend development deals with the part of the application that users interact with. It includes everything the user sees and uses, such as buttons, text fields, images, navigation menus, and overall layout. A full stack developer must be skilled in using HTML, CSS, and JavaScript to structure, style, and add interactivity to the user interface (UI). Additionally, in modern web development, frameworks like React, Angular, or Vue.js are commonly used to build responsive and efficient UIs.

Key frontend technologies include:

- **HTML (Hypertext Markup Language):** The skeleton or structure of a webpage, defining the elements that are displayed.

- **CSS (Cascading Style Sheets):** Styling language that controls the appearance of HTML elements, such as colors, fonts, and layout.
- **JavaScript:** The scripting language that enables dynamic content, such as animations, form validation, and interactive features.

In addition to these basic technologies, frontend developers often work with APIs (Application Programming Interfaces) to fetch data from the backend and display it to the user. This interaction between the frontend and backend is critical to the user experience.

Backend Development

Backend development focuses on what happens behind the scenes of an application. It handles the server, database, and application logic, including tasks like user authentication, data storage, and processing requests from the frontend. A full stack developer working on the backend must be proficient in server-side programming languages such as Java, Python, Ruby, or Node.js.

Key backend responsibilities include:

- **Database Management:** Storing and retrieving data from databases like MySQL, PostgreSQL, MongoDB, or Oracle.
- **Server-Side Logic:** Writing the business logic that governs how data is processed and returned to the frontend.
- **APIs (Application Programming Interfaces):** Building endpoints for the frontend to interact with, typically using REST or GraphQL.
- **Security and Authentication:** Implementing features such as encryption, token-based authentication (e.g., JWT), and securing APIs against attacks like SQL injection and cross-site scripting (XSS).

Backend developers often need to understand how to scale applications to handle more users and requests efficiently, which may involve the use of caching, load balancing, and server optimizations.

Why Full Stack Development?

Full stack development is particularly valuable in today's fast-paced software industry for several reasons:

1. **Efficiency:** Full stack developers can work on both the frontend and backend of an application, reducing the need for communication between multiple developers or teams.
2. **Versatility:** Full stack developers can handle various tasks, from designing a website's layout to managing the backend logic that supports it. This flexibility can be critical in small teams or startups.
3. **Cost-Effective:** Hiring a full stack developer can be more cost-effective for businesses since they don't need to hire separate specialists for frontend and backend development.
4. **Better Coordination:** A full stack developer has a holistic understanding of how the frontend and backend of an application work together, which helps in creating a cohesive and optimized final product.

Why Choose Spring Boot 3 and React?

Spring Boot and **React** have become popular choices for full stack development because they are highly efficient, scalable, and enable developers to build robust applications that are both user-friendly and performant.

Spring Boot 3

Spring Boot is a framework for building Java-based applications quickly and efficiently. It is an extension of the Spring Framework, providing a simplified and streamlined approach to building production-grade applications. **Spring Boot 3**, the latest version, introduces several new features and improvements that make it even more compelling for backend development.

Key features of Spring Boot 3 include:

- **Microservice Architecture Support:** Spring Boot is ideal for building microservices, which are independently deployable services that communicate with each other. This architecture is favored for its scalability and ease of management in large systems.
- **REST API Development:** Spring Boot simplifies the process of creating RESTful APIs, allowing the backend to communicate with frontend applications.

- **Spring Security Integration:** Built-in security features such as authentication, authorization, and protection against common security threats (e.g., CSRF, XSS) make Spring Boot a strong choice for secure applications.
- **Auto-Configuration:** Spring Boot's auto-configuration feature automatically configures the necessary components based on your application's dependencies, drastically reducing the amount of manual setup required.

React

React, developed by Facebook, is a powerful JavaScript library for building dynamic, interactive user interfaces. It has quickly become one of the most popular frontend frameworks due to its simplicity, performance, and large ecosystem.

Key features of React include:

- **Component-Based Architecture:** React applications are built using reusable components, which promotes code reusability and simplifies the development process.
- **Virtual DOM:** React uses a Virtual DOM, which allows for efficient rendering of changes in the UI without requiring the entire page to reload. This makes applications fast and responsive.
- **React Hooks:** Introduced in React 16.8, hooks such as useState and useEffect allow developers to manage state and side effects in functional components, simplifying code and making it easier to maintain.
- **Strong Ecosystem:** With tools like React Router for handling routing and libraries like Redux for state management, React offers a comprehensive ecosystem for building scalable frontend applications.

Why Use Spring Boot 3 and React Together?

The combination of **Spring Boot** for backend development and **React** for frontend development provides a powerful full stack solution. Some reasons to choose this combination include:

- **Separation of Concerns:** Spring Boot and React allow for a clean separation between the backend (business logic, data processing) and the frontend (user interface), making it easier to develop and maintain the application.
- **Scalability:** Both Spring Boot and React are highly scalable, making this stack ideal for applications that need to grow in terms of users and data.
- **Rapid Development:** Spring Boot's auto-configuration and React's component-based architecture help speed up the development process by reducing boilerplate code and allowing for more focus on core functionality.
- **Strong Community Support:** Both Spring Boot and React have active communities that provide extensive documentation, tutorials, and third-party libraries, which can accelerate development and troubleshooting.

Overview of the Book's Structure and Approach

This book is structured to provide a comprehensive understanding of full stack development using **Spring Boot 3** and **React**. The aim is to guide readers from setting up their development environment to building complex, scalable applications. Throughout the book, we will cover both the theoretical concepts and practical applications, ensuring readers gain the skills necessary to build real-world projects.

Key Features of the Book:

1. **Hands-On Projects:** Each chapter will introduce new concepts and guide you through building a fully functional project, reinforcing your understanding through practice.
2. **Comprehensive Coverage:** We will cover everything from setting up your environment to deploying your full stack application, ensuring you have the knowledge to handle both the frontend and backend.
3. **Best Practices and Optimization:** In addition to building applications, this book emphasizes best practices, including security, performance optimization, and testing.

5

4. **Focus on Modern Tools:** We will use the latest versions of Spring Boot (3.x) and React (18+), ensuring you are working with up-to-date tools and frameworks.

5. **Testing and Deployment:** We will guide you through testing your applications and deploying them to the cloud, ensuring they are production-ready.

Setting up Your Development Environment

Before diving into full stack development with Spring Boot 3 and React, it's essential to have your development environment set up properly. This section will guide you through installing the necessary tools and configuring your environment to ensure a smooth development process.

Required Tools and Technologies

1. **Java 17:** The latest LTS (Long-Term Support) version of Java.
2. **Spring Boot 3:** Backend framework for building REST APIs and microservices.
3. **Node.js and npm:** JavaScript runtime and package manager used for React.
4. **IDE (Integrated Development Environment):** VS Code or IntelliJ IDEA.
5. **Git:** Version control system to manage your codebase.

Installing Java, Spring Boot, Node.js, and npm

Installing Java

Java is the foundation for Spring Boot, so installing the correct version is crucial. We'll be using **Java 17**, which is the current LTS version.

1. **Download Java 17:**

- Go to the official Oracle website and download the Java 17 JDK (Java

Development Kit).
- Follow the installation instructions for your operating system (Windows, macOS, or Linux).

1. **Verify Installation:**

- Open your terminal or command prompt and type the following command to verify the installation:

```
java -version
```

- You should see the output displaying Java 17.

Installing Spring Boot

Spring Boot can be easily installed using **Spring Initializr**, an online tool that helps generate Spring Boot projects with the necessary dependencies.

1. **Generate a Spring Boot Project:**

- Visit **https://start.spring.io/**.
- Select the latest version of Spring Boot (3.x).
- Choose **Maven Project**, set the language to **Java**, and specify **JDK 17**.
- Add dependencies such as **Spring Web** (for REST APIs) and **Spring Data JPA** (for database connectivity).
- Download the generated project.

1. **Building and Running the Spring Boot Application:**

- Open the downloaded project in your IDE (e.g., IntelliJ IDEA).
- Build the project using Maven or Gradle.

- Run the application to verify that Spring Boot is set up correctly.

Installing Node.js and npm

Node.js is required for running the React development environment, and npm is the package manager used to install and manage dependencies.

1. **Download and Install Node.js:**

- Visit the official Node.js website (**https://nodejs.org**) and download the latest LTS version.
- Follow the installation instructions for your operating system.

1. **Verify Installation:**

- Open your terminal or command prompt and type the following commands to verify the installation:

```
node -v
npm -v
```

- You should see the version numbers for both Node.js and npm.

1. **Installing Create React App:** Create React App is a tool that sets up a new React project with all the necessary configurations.

- Install it globally by running the following command:

```lua
npm install -g create-react-app
```

- Verify the installation by creating a new React project:

```lua
create-react-app my-app
```

- Navigate to the project directory and start the development server:

```bash
cd my-app
npm start
```

Setting Up IDE (VS Code/IntelliJ IDEA)

Choosing the right Integrated Development Environment (IDE) is crucial for efficient coding. Both **VS Code** and **IntelliJ IDEA** are widely used in full stack development.

Visual Studio Code (VS Code)

VS Code is a lightweight, open-source code editor with robust support for JavaScript, React, and Java.

1. **Download and Install VS Code:**

- Go to the official VS Code website and download the appropriate version for your operating system.

- Install the editor following the platform-specific instructions.

1. **Install Extensions for Java and React Development:**

- **Java Extension Pack:** Provides support for Java development in VS Code.
- **Spring Boot Extension Pack:** Adds support for Spring Boot development.
- **ESLint and Prettier:** Ensure consistent code formatting and error checking in your React code.

IntelliJ IDEA

IntelliJ IDEA is a popular IDE for Java development and has excellent integration with Spring Boot and frontend technologies like React.

1. **Download and Install IntelliJ IDEA:**

- Visit JetBrains' website and download IntelliJ IDEA (Community or Ultimate edition).
- Install it by following the instructions for your operating system.

1. **Install Plugins:**

- **Spring Boot Plugin:** Adds support for Spring Boot applications.
- **Node.js Plugin:** Enables Node.js and React development within IntelliJ.

Version Control with Git

Version control is essential for managing code changes and collaborating with other developers. **Git** is the most popular version control system, allowing you to track changes, revert to previous versions, and collaborate on code through platforms like GitHub and GitLab.

Installing Git

1. **Download Git:**

- Visit the official Git website (**https://git-scm.com/**) and download the latest version.
- Follow the installation instructions for your operating system.

1. **Verify Installation:**

- Open your terminal or command prompt and type the following command to verify the installation:

```css
git --version
```

Basic Git Commands

- ### **Cloning a Repository:**

```bash
git clone [repository-url]
```

- ### **Adding Changes to Staging:**

```csharp
git add .
```

- **Committing Changes:**

```sql
git commit -m "commit message"
```

- **Pushing Changes to a Remote Repository:**

```css
git push origin main
```

- **Pulling Changes from a Remote Repository:**

```css
git pull origin main
```

By mastering these tools and setting up your development environment, you'll be ready to start building full stack applications with Spring Boot 3 and React.

Chapter 2: Spring Boot 3 Fundamentals

Spring Boot is a highly popular framework designed to simplify Java development, especially when it comes to creating microservices, REST APIs, and enterprise-grade applications. With the release of Spring Boot 3, developers have access to new features, improvements in performance, and enhanced capabilities that further streamline the development process.

I n this chapter, we'll dive deep into the fundamentals of **Spring Boot 3**, covering everything from setting up your first application to exploring key features like annotations, dependency injection, and RESTful API development. By the end of this chapter, you'll have a solid understanding of how Spring Boot 3 works and be able to create your own backend systems.

Overview of Spring Boot Framework

Spring Boot is an extension of the Spring Framework, which has been widely adopted for building enterprise applications in Java. While the Spring Framework is highly powerful, it comes with a significant amount of configuration, which can be daunting for developers, especially when building new applications from scratch. Spring Boot simplifies this by offering an opinionated view of Spring, reducing the need for extensive configuration, and providing ready-to-use production-grade applications.

Key Benefits of Spring Boot

1. **Auto-Configuration:** Spring Boot automatically configures many parts of your application based on the libraries and dependencies you include. This allows you to focus more on writing business logic rather than boilerplate configuration.

2. **Embedded Servers:** Spring Boot applications come with embedded web servers such as **Tomcat** and **Jetty**, which allow you to package and run your application without the need for external servers.

3. **Microservice-Ready:** With built-in support for microservices architecture, Spring Boot makes it easier to create modular, scalable services that can interact with one another.

4. **Spring Ecosystem Integration:** Spring Boot seamlessly integrates with other Spring modules, such as **Spring Data**, **Spring Security**, and **Spring Cloud**, allowing you to build complex applications with ease.
5. **Production-Ready Features:** Spring Boot includes features such as **Actuator** for monitoring, health checks, and metrics out of the box, making it easier to manage applications in production.

Creating Your First Spring Boot 3 Application

Getting started with Spring Boot 3 is incredibly simple, thanks to the **Spring Initializr**, which allows you to generate a pre-configured project with the dependencies you need. In this section, we'll walk through the steps to create your first Spring Boot 3 application.

Step 1: Using Spring Initializr

1. **Go to Spring Initializr:**

- Open your browser and visit https://start.spring.io/.

1. **Select Project Configuration:**

- **Project Type:** Choose **Maven Project**.
- **Language:** Select **Java**.
- **Spring Boot Version:** Ensure you select the latest **3.x** version.
- **Group:** This is typically the package name for your project, such as com.example.
- **Artifact:** This is the name of your project, such as myapp.

1. **Add Dependencies:**

- Add the following essential dependencies to get started:
- **Spring Web**: For creating RESTful web services.
- **Spring Data JPA**: For database interaction and ORM (Object Relational Mapping).

- **H2 Database**: A lightweight in-memory database for testing purposes.

1. **Generate the Project:**

- Click **Generate**, and your project will be downloaded as a ZIP file. Extract it to a folder of your choice.

Step 2: Importing the Project into Your IDE

1. **Open your IDE** (e.g., IntelliJ IDEA or VS Code) and import the Maven project you just generated.
2. **Build the project** using Maven to ensure all dependencies are downloaded and the project structure is correctly set up.

Step 3: Running the Application

1. Once the project is imported, locate the **Application.java** file in the src/main/java directory. This file contains the main() method, which is the entry point to your Spring Boot application.
2. Run the **Application.java** file as a Java application. The embedded server (e.g., Tomcat) will start, and you'll see the application running in your console.

Your Spring Boot 3 application is now up and running!

Spring Boot 3 New Features and Updates

Spring Boot 3 introduces several new features and improvements that make it more powerful, secure, and efficient. Below are some key updates:

1. GraalVM Native Image Support

GraalVM is a high-performance runtime that provides significant improvements in startup time and memory usage for Java applications. With Spring Boot 3, it is now possible to compile Spring applications into **native images** using GraalVM, allowing them to run with minimal overhead, making them ideal for microservices or cloud-native environments.

2. Improved Security Features

Spring Boot 3 comes with updated support for **Spring Security** 6.0, which includes:

- **OAuth2 Support:** Enhanced support for OAuth2, including integrations with common identity providers (e.g., Google, Facebook).
- **Security Filters:** New security filters that make it easier to configure custom authentication and authorization mechanisms.

3. Observability and Monitoring

With the increased importance of monitoring in cloud environments, Spring Boot 3 integrates with **Micrometer** for observability. Micrometer provides a simple facade for monitoring systems such as **Prometheus** and **Grafana**, enabling better visibility into your application's performance and health.

4. Web Framework Enhancements

The **Spring Web** module in Spring Boot 3 has been optimized to support **HTTP/2**, which provides faster, more efficient communication between the client and server. Additionally, **WebSockets** have been improved for real-time applications.

Understanding Annotations and Dependency Injection

Annotations are a key feature of Spring Boot that simplify the development process by allowing developers to configure components declaratively. Spring Boot uses several annotations that automatically configure and wire up components, significantly reducing the amount of boilerplate code needed.

1. @SpringBootApplication

This is one of the most important annotations in Spring Boot. It is typically placed on the main class of your application (the class containing the main() method) and serves as a meta-annotation, combining:

- **@EnableAutoConfiguration:** Enables Spring Boot's auto-configuration feature, which configures your application based on the dependencies added.

- **@ComponentScan:** Tells Spring Boot to scan the specified package for components, configurations, and services.
- **@Configuration:** Indicates that the class is a source of bean definitions for the Spring container.

```java
@SpringBootApplication
public class MyApp {
    public static void main(String[] args) {
        SpringApplication.run(MyApp.class, args);
    }
}
```

2. @RestController

This annotation is used to define a controller in Spring Boot that handles HTTP requests and responses. It is commonly used in REST APIs to map incoming requests to methods that return data (typically in JSON format).

```java
@RestController
public class HelloController {
    @GetMapping("/hello")
    public String sayHello() {
        return "Hello, World!";
    }
}
```

3. @Autowired

Spring Boot uses **Dependency Injection (DI)** to manage the lifecycle of beans. The **@Autowired** annotation is used to automatically inject dependencies into a class. It can be applied to constructors, methods, or fields.

```java
@Service
public class MyService {
    private final MyRepository repository;

    @Autowired
    public MyService(MyRepository repository) {
        this.repository = repository;
    }

    public List<MyEntity> getAllEntities() {
        return repository.findAll();
    }
}
```

4. @Service, @Repository, and @Component

These annotations define the roles of specific classes in your application:

- **@Service:** Marks a class as a service, indicating it contains business logic.
- **@Repository:** Indicates that the class interacts with the database, typically through Spring Data JPA or other persistence mechanisms.
- **@Component:** Marks a generic Spring-managed component.

Building RESTful APIs with Spring Boot

One of the core use cases of Spring Boot is to build **RESTful APIs**, which allow the backend to communicate with the frontend by exchanging data over HTTP. REST (Representational State Transfer) is an architectural style that uses HTTP methods to perform CRUD (Create, Read, Update, Delete) operations on resources.

1. Understanding REST and HTTP Methods

In a RESTful API, resources are typically represented as entities (e.g., users, products, orders) that can be manipulated using the following HTTP methods:

- **GET:** Retrieve data from the server.
- **POST:** Submit data to the server, usually to create a new resource.

- **PUT/PATCH:** Update an existing resource.
- **DELETE:** Remove a resource from the server.

For example, to manage a list of users in a REST API, you might have the following endpoints:

- GET /users: Retrieve a list of all users.
- POST /users: Create a new user.
- PUT /users/{id}: Update an existing user with the specified ID.
- DELETE /users/{id}: Delete a user with the specified ID.

2. Building a Simple REST API

Let's build a basic REST API for managing a list of users using Spring Boot.

Step 1: Create a Model First, define a **User** model class that represents the user entity.

```java
public class User {
    private Long id;
    private String name;
    private String email;

    // Getters and Setters
}
```

Step 2: Create a Controller Next, create a controller class to handle the HTTP requests for managing users.

```
@RestController
@RequestMapping("/users")
public class UserController {

    private List<User> users = new ArrayList<>();
```

```
@GetMapping
public List<User> getAllUsers() {
    return users;
}

@PostMapping
public User createUser(@RequestBody User user) {
    users.add(user);
    return user;
}

@PutMapping("/{id}")
public User updateUser(@PathVariable Long id, @RequestBody
User updatedUser) {
    for (User user : users) {
        if (user.getId().equals(id)) {
            user.setName(updatedUser.getName());
            user.setEmail(updatedUser.getEmail());
            return user;
        }
    }
    return null;
}

@DeleteMapping("/{id}")
public void deleteUser(@PathVariable Long id) {
    users.removeIf(user -> user.getId().equals(id));
}
}
```

In this example, the UserController class handles requests to the /users endpoint. It provides basic CRUD functionality for managing users, including getting all users, creating a new user, updating an existing user, and deleting a user.

3. Connecting to a Database with Spring Data JPA

While the previous example used an in-memory list to store users, in a real-world application, you'll typically interact with a database. Spring Boot simplifies this with **Spring Data JPA**, which provides an abstraction layer over traditional JDBC.

Step 1: Create a Repository Create a repository interface for the **User** entity by extending the JpaRepository interface. Spring Data JPA will automatically provide implementations for basic CRUD operations.

```java

@Repository
public interface UserRepository extends JpaRepository<User, Long> {
}
```

Step 2: Update the Service and Controller Now, update the service and controller to use the repository instead of the in-memory list. This will enable the API to persist user data to a database, such as H2 or MySQL.

Conclusion

This chapter has covered the core concepts of **Spring Boot 3**, from setting up your first application to building RESTful APIs and understanding key features like dependency injection, annotations, and Spring Data JPA. With this foundational knowledge, you're ready to start building robust backend systems that can integrate seamlessly with the frontend, laying the groundwork for full stack development. In the next chapter, we will explore React, the frontend technology that complements Spring Boot, enabling you to build dynamic and interactive user interfaces.

Chapter 3: React Fundamentals

React is a powerful JavaScript library for building user interfaces, especially for single-page applications (SPAs). It enables developers to create dynamic, responsive UIs with ease, while focusing on efficient rendering and state management. In this chapter, we will dive deep into the fundamentals of React, covering key concepts such as JSX, components, state, props, hooks, and routing. By the end of this chapter, you will have a strong understanding of React and how it can be used to build the frontend of a full stack application when paired with Spring Boot.

I ntroduction to React and the Virtual DOM

React was developed by Facebook and has quickly become one of the most widely adopted frontend libraries. One of the primary reasons for its popularity is its **Virtual DOM**, which optimizes the process of updating the UI and improves the overall performance of web applications.

What is the DOM?

The **DOM (Document Object Model)** is a representation of the structure and content of a web page. Every time the user interacts with a web page (such as clicking a button or submitting a form), the browser updates the DOM to reflect those changes. However, updating the actual DOM can be slow and inefficient, especially when dealing with complex UIs that involve many elements.

What is the Virtual DOM?

React introduces the concept of the **Virtual DOM**, which is a lightweight, in-memory representation of the actual DOM. When changes are made in a React application, React updates the Virtual DOM first. Then, it compares the Virtual DOM with the real DOM (a process called "diffing") and updates only the parts of the actual DOM that have changed. This process is significantly faster than updating the entire DOM, resulting in improved performance and a more responsive UI.

Setting Up Your First React Application with Create React App

To get started with React, we'll use **Create React App (CRA)**, a tool that sets up a new React project with all the necessary configurations and dependencies. CRA is the fastest and easiest way to bootstrap a new React application without having to configure Webpack, Babel, or other build tools manually.

Step 1: Installing Create React App

Before creating a new React application, ensure that you have **Node.js** and **npm** installed. You can verify this by running the following commands in your terminal:

```bash

node -v
npm -v
```

If Node.js and npm are not installed, download and install them from the official Node.js website. Once installed, you can install Create React App globally by running the following command:

```bash

npm install -g create-react-app
```

Step 2: Creating a New React Application

After installing Create React App, you can create a new React project by running the following command:

```bash

create-react-app my-app
```

This command generates a new folder called my-app containing the basic structure of a React project. Once the project is created, navigate into the project directory:

```bash
bash

cd my-app
```

Step 3: Running the Application

To start the development server and run the application, execute the following command:

```bash
bash

npm start
```

This will open your new React application in the browser at http://localhost: 3000/. The default Create React App template includes a simple "Welcome to React" page, which you can modify to start building your own application.

JSX: Combining HTML and JavaScript

In React, you define the structure of your UI using **JSX (JavaScript XML)**. JSX is a syntax extension for JavaScript that allows you to write HTML-like code directly within your JavaScript files. While JSX may look like HTML, it is actually compiled into JavaScript by React before being rendered to the DOM.

Why Use JSX?

JSX provides a clear and concise way to define UI components, making your code more readable and maintainable. By combining JavaScript and HTML-like syntax, JSX enables you to easily embed dynamic content and logic directly within your UI definitions.

Basic JSX Example

```jsx
jsx

function Welcome() {
  return <h1>Hello, world!</h1>;
}
```

In this example, the Welcome function returns a JSX element (<h1>Hello, world!</h1>) that will be rendered as an HTML <h1> element. While this may look like HTML, it is actually JSX, which will be converted to a JavaScript React.createElement() call behind the scenes.

Embedding JavaScript Expressions in JSX

You can embed JavaScript expressions directly within JSX using curly braces {}. This allows you to dynamically render content based on variables, functions, or expressions.

```jsx
function Greeting(props) {
  return <h1>Hello, {props.name}!</h1>;
}
```

In this example, the Greeting component accepts a name prop and dynamically inserts it into the JSX element.

JSX Must Return a Single Element

One important rule to remember is that JSX must return a single element. If you want to return multiple elements, you can wrap them in a parent element such as a <div> or use React fragments (<> ... </>) to avoid adding unnecessary HTML elements to the DOM.

```jsx
function App() {
  return (
    <>
      <h1>Welcome</h1>
      <p>This is a React application.</p>
    </>
  );
}
```

React Components: Functional vs. Class Components

React applications are built using **components**, which are reusable pieces of

UI. Components can be written as either **functional components** or **class components**, though functional components have become the preferred choice in modern React development, especially with the introduction of **React Hooks**.

Functional Components

A **functional component** is a JavaScript function that returns JSX. Functional components are simple, stateless, and easy to write, making them ideal for most use cases.

```jsx
function Welcome() {
  return <h1>Welcome to React!</h1>;
}
```

Class Components

A **class component** is a more complex type of component that extends the React.Component class. Class components can manage their own internal state and lifecycle methods, but with the introduction of hooks, class components are being used less frequently.

```jsx
class Welcome extends React.Component {
  render() {
    return <h1>Welcome to React!</h1>;
  }
}
```

When to Use Functional Components vs. Class Components

- **Functional Components** are preferred for their simplicity and ease of use. They are sufficient for most use cases, especially when paired with hooks for state management and side effects.
- **Class Components** are used when more advanced features, such as

lifecycle methods or state management, are required. However, with the advent of hooks, functional components are often capable of handling the same tasks with less code and complexity.

Props: Passing Data Between Components

Props (short for properties) are a mechanism for passing data from a parent component to a child component. In React, props are read-only and cannot be modified by the child component. This ensures that the data flow in a React application is unidirectional, meaning that data always flows from parent to child.

Passing Props to a Component

You can pass props to a component by adding attributes to the component tag when rendering it.

```jsx
function Greeting(props) {
  return <h1>Hello, {props.name}!</h1>;
}

function App() {
  return <Greeting name="Alice" />;
}
```

In this example, the App component passes a name prop to the Greeting component, which renders it as part of the greeting message.

Using Props in a Functional Component

In functional components, props are passed as an argument to the component function and can be accessed directly within the JSX.

```jsx
function Greeting({ name }) {
  return <h1>Hello, {name}!</h1>;
}
```

State: Managing Dynamic Data

While props are useful for passing data from parent to child, they are static and cannot be changed by the component. For components that need to manage dynamic data, React provides **state**.

Using State in Functional Components with useState Hook

In functional components, state is managed using the **useState** hook. The useState hook allows you to define a state variable and a function to update that state.

```jsx
import React, { useState } from 'react';

function Counter() {
  const [count, setCount] = useState(0);

  return (
    <div>
      <p>You clicked {count} times</p>
      <button onClick={() => setCount(count + 1)}>Click me</button>
    </div>
  );
}
```

In this example, the Counter component uses the useState hook to manage the count state variable. When the button is clicked, the setCount function is called to update the state, which triggers a re-render of the component with the updated count value.

useState Syntax

- The useState hook takes an initial state value as an argument and returns an array containing the current state value and a function to update that state.
- The state update function (setCount in this case) can be called to modify the state and trigger a re-render of the component.

React Hooks: Managing Side Effects with useEffect

One of the most important hooks in React is **useEffect**, which allows you to manage **side effects** in functional components. Side effects include things like fetching data from an API, updating the DOM, or setting up timers, all of which occur outside the normal flow of rendering.

Basic useEffect Example

```jsx
import React, { useState, useEffect } from 'react';

function Timer() {
  const [seconds, setSeconds] = useState(0);

  useEffect(() => {
    const interval = setInterval(() => {
      setSeconds(seconds => seconds + 1);
    }, 1000);

    return () => clearInterval(interval); // Cleanup on component
    unmount
  }, []);

  return <p>{seconds} seconds have passed.</p>;
}
```

In this example, the useEffect hook is used to set up a timer that increments the seconds state variable every second. The effect runs after the component renders and continues to run on every re-render. The cleanup function (clearInterval) ensures that the interval is cleared when the component is unmounted, preventing memory leaks.

useEffect Syntax

- The useEffect hook takes two arguments: a function that contains the side effect and an optional dependency array.
- The dependency array specifies when the effect should be re-run. If the array is empty ([]), the effect will only run once when the component

mounts. If the array contains state or props, the effect will run whenever those values change.

Handling Forms and User Input in React

Handling forms and user input is a common task in any web application. React makes it easy to manage form elements and update state based on user input.

Controlled Components

In React, form elements such as <input> and <textarea> can be **controlled components**, meaning their value is controlled by React state. A controlled component's value is updated based on user input, and the component re-renders when the state changes.

```jsx
function Form() {
  const [name, setName] = useState('');

  const handleChange = (event) => {
    setName(event.target.value);
  };

  return (
    <form>
      <label>
        Name:
        <input type="text" value={name} onChange={handleChange} />
      </label>
      <p>Your name is: {name}</p>
    </form>
  );
}
```

In this example, the input element's value is controlled by the name state. As the user types into the input field, the handleChange function updates the state, causing the component to re-render with the new value.

Handling Form Submissions

To handle form submissions, you can add an onSubmit handler to the form element.

```jsx
function Form() {
  const [name, setName] = useState('');

  const handleSubmit = (event) => {
    event.preventDefault();
    alert(`Form submitted with name: ${name}`);
  };

  return (
    <form onSubmit={handleSubmit}>
      <label>
        Name:
        <input type="text" value={name} onChange={(e) =>
        setName(e.target.value)} />
      </label>
      <button type="submit">Submit</button>
    </form>
  );
}
```

In this example, when the form is submitted, the handleSubmit function is called, which prevents the default form submission behavior (which would reload the page) and instead displays an alert with the form data.

Routing in React with React Router

As your React application grows, you may need to add multiple pages or views. React handles routing using a third-party library called **React Router**, which enables navigation between different components without reloading the entire page.

Installing React Router

To get started with React Router, you need to install the package:

```bash
bash

npm install react-router-dom
```

Setting Up Basic Routes

Once React Router is installed, you can define routes using the Browser-Router, Route, and Link components.

```jsx
jsx

import { BrowserRouter as Router, Route, Link, Switch } from
'react-router-dom';

function Home() {
  return <h2>Home</h2>;
}

function About() {
  return <h2>About</h2>;
}

function App() {
  return (
    <Router>
      <nav>
        <Link to="/">Home</Link>
        <Link to="/about">About</Link>
      </nav>

      <Switch>
        <Route path="/" exact component={Home} />
        <Route path="/about" component={About} />
      </Switch>
    </Router>
  );
}
```

In this example, the Router component wraps the entire application and defines the available routes. The Link components allow the user to navigate between the Home and About components without refreshing the page.

Dynamic Routing

You can also define dynamic routes with React Router by using route parameters.

```jsx
function User({ match }) {
  return <h2>User ID: {match.params.id}</h2>;
}

function App() {
  return (
    <Router>
      <Switch>
        <Route path="/user/:id" component={User} />
      </Switch>
    </Router>
  );
}
```

In this example, the User component will receive the id parameter from the URL, which can be accessed via match.params.id.

Conclusion

This chapter covered the fundamentals of React, including setting up a React application, understanding JSX, building components, managing state and props, using hooks like useState and useEffect, handling forms, and implementing routing with React Router. With these building blocks, you now have the foundation to build dynamic, interactive UIs with React.

In the next chapter, we'll explore how to connect React with a Spring Boot backend, allowing you to build full stack applications that combine the best of both frontend and backend development.

Chapter 4: Connecting Frontend and Backend

Building full-stack applications often involves connecting a frontend, which handles user interface and interactions, to a backend that processes data, communicates with a database, and serves the necessary information. With React on the frontend and Spring Boot on the backend, you are equipped to create powerful, scalable applications.

I n this chapter, we will explore how to efficiently connect React with a Spring Boot backend, ensuring smooth communication between the client and server using RESTful APIs. You will learn how to fetch data from the backend, handle asynchronous operations, and manage frontend-backend state synchronization. We'll also cover best practices for working with APIs, such as error handling, data caching, and security.

Understanding REST API Integration

Before we dive into the technical aspects, it is essential to understand how data flows between the frontend and backend. In full-stack applications, the frontend communicates with the backend via **APIs (Application Programming Interfaces)**. Specifically, RESTful APIs are one of the most commonly used paradigms in web development.

What is a REST API?

REST (Representational State Transfer) is an architectural style for designing networked applications. RESTful APIs are stateless and use standard HTTP methods to interact with resources. These methods include:

- **GET:** Retrieve data from the server (e.g., fetching user details).
- **POST:** Send data to the server (e.g., creating a new resource).
- **PUT:** Update an existing resource on the server.
- **DELETE:** Remove a resource from the server.

For instance, in a social media app, you might use a GET request to fetch user profiles from the backend and display them on the frontend, or a POST request to submit a new post from the user.

HTTP Methods and CRUD Operations

In the context of full-stack development, REST APIs are often designed to perform **CRUD (Create, Read, Update, Delete)** operations. The HTTP methods correspond to these operations as follows:

- **GET:** Read data (retrieve resources).
- **POST:** Create a new resource.
- **PUT or PATCH:** Update an existing resource.
- **DELETE:** Remove an existing resource.

Each of these methods interacts with **endpoints**, which are specific URLs that the frontend can access to perform an operation. For example:

- GET /api/users: Fetches a list of users.
- POST /api/users: Creates a new user.
- PUT /api/users/{id}: Updates a user with the specified ID.
- DELETE /api/users/{id}: Deletes a user with the specified ID.

JSON: The Standard Data Format

When building a full-stack application with React and Spring Boot, the data exchanged between the frontend and backend is typically in **JSON (JavaScript Object Notation)** format. JSON is lightweight, human-readable, and easy for both machines and humans to parse.

Fetching Data in React with Fetch API and Axios

To retrieve data from a Spring Boot backend, React offers several options for making HTTP requests. The two most common tools are the **Fetch API** and **Axios**.

1. Fetch API

The **Fetch API** is a built-in JavaScript function for making network requests. It is simple, promises-based, and available in all modern browsers.

Basic Fetch Example

```javascript
useEffect(() => {
  fetch('http://localhost:8080/api/users')
    .then(response => response.json())
    .then(data => setUsers(data))
    .catch(error => console.error('Error fetching users:', error));
}, []);
```

In this example, we use the fetch() function to make a GET request to the /api/users endpoint of the Spring Boot backend. Once the data is received and parsed into JSON, it is stored in the users state variable.

2. Axios

Axios is an external library that simplifies making HTTP requests. It provides several advantages over the Fetch API, including automatic JSON parsing, better error handling, and support for request/response interceptors.

To use Axios, you first need to install it via npm:

```bash
npm install axios
```

Basic Axios Example

```javascript
import axios from 'axios';

useEffect(() => {
  axios.get('http://localhost:8080/api/users')
    .then(response => setUsers(response.data))
    .catch(error => console.error('Error fetching users:', error));
}, []);
```

In this example, Axios performs the same GET request as the Fetch API, but the code is more concise, and error handling is easier to manage. Axios also supports advanced features like request retries, request cancellation, and custom headers.

Choosing Between Fetch API and Axios

- **Fetch API:** Great for simple requests and built directly into the browser.
- **Axios:** Ideal for more complex applications requiring features such as request cancellation, automatic retries, or advanced response formatting.

Handling Asynchronous Operations

Fetching data from an API is an inherently asynchronous operation. The browser doesn't know when the response from the server will arrive, so it doesn't block other code from executing. Instead, it uses promises to handle the operation, where the code waits for the promise to resolve or reject (success or failure).

Using Promises

Promises provide a cleaner syntax for handling asynchronous operations compared to traditional callback functions. A promise represents the eventual completion (or failure) of an asynchronous operation and its resulting value.

Promise Example with Fetch

```javascript
fetch('http://localhost:8080/api/users')
  .then(response => response.json())
  .then(data => console.log(data))
  .catch(error => console.error('Error:', error));
```

In this example, fetch() returns a promise. Once the promise is resolved, the code proceeds to the .then() block where the data is processed. If an error occurs during the fetch operation, the promise is rejected, and the .catch() block handles the error.

Using Async/Await

An alternative to using .then() is the **async/await** syntax, which simplifies promise-based code. It allows you to write asynchronous code that looks synchronous, making it easier to read and maintain.

Async/Await Example

```javascript
const fetchUsers = async () => {
  try {
    const response = await
    fetch('http://localhost:8080/api/users');
    const data = await response.json();
    setUsers(data);
  } catch (error) {
    console.error('Error fetching users:', error);
  }
};

useEffect(() => {
  fetchUsers();
}, []);
```

In this example, await is used to pause the execution of the function until the fetch request completes, at which point the data is returned. If an error occurs, the code jumps to the catch block to handle it. This approach makes the code more readable and easier to understand, especially for complex operations.

Managing Global State with Context API

As your React application grows, you may need to manage state across multiple components, especially when dealing with data fetched from the backend. **Context API** provides a way to share state between components without passing props down manually at every level.

What is the Context API?

The Context API allows you to create a **context** object that can be accessed by any component within your application, bypassing the need to pass props manually through every component.

Creating a Context

```javascript
const UserContext = React.createContext();

function App() {
  const [users, setUsers] = useState([]);

  return (
    <UserContext.Provider value={{ users, setUsers }}>
      <UserList />
    </UserContext.Provider>
  );
}
```

In this example, the UserContext.Provider component wraps the UserList component, making the users and setUsers state available to any component within the UserContext tree.

Accessing Context in Child Components

```javascript
function UserList() {
  const { users } = useContext(UserContext);

  return (
    <div>
      {users.map(user => (
        <div key={user.id}>{user.name}</div>
      ))}
    </div>
  );
}
```

Here, the useContext() hook is used to access the users state from the UserContext. This allows the UserList component to display the list of users without needing to pass the users state as a prop.

When to Use the Context API

The Context API is ideal for managing global state that needs to be accessible by multiple components, such as:

- Authentication status.
- User data.
- Theme settings.
- Application-wide configurations.

While the Context API is powerful, it should be used sparingly, as it can make debugging and testing more difficult if overused.

Sending POST Requests and Handling Form Submissions

In addition to fetching data from the backend, you will also need to send data from the frontend to the backend, typically using **POST requests**. This is often required when creating new resources, such as submitting a form to create a new user or product.

Handling Form Submissions in React

React provides a straightforward way to manage form inputs and send the form data to the backend. Let's walk through an example of submitting a user registration form to the Spring Boot backend.

Basic Form Example

```javascript
function UserForm() {
  const [name, setName] = useState('');
  const [email, setEmail] = useState('');

  const handleSubmit = async (e) => {
    e.preventDefault();

    const userData = { name, email };

    try {
      const response = await
      fetch('http://localhost:8080/api/users', {
        method: 'POST',
```

```
      headers: {
        'Content-Type': 'application/json',
      },
      body: JSON.stringify(userData),
    });

    if (response.ok) {
      console.log('User created successfully');
    } else {
      console.error('Error creating user');
    }
  } catch (error) {
    console.error('Error:', error);
  }
};

return (
  <form onSubmit={handleSubmit}>
    <div>
      <label>Name:</label>
      <input
        type="text"
        value={name}
        onChange={(e) => setName(e.target.value)}
      />
    </div>
    <div>
      <label>Email:</label>
      <input
        type="email"
        value={email}
        onChange={(e) => setEmail(e.target.value)}
      />
    </div>
    <button type="submit">Submit</button>
  </form>
);
}
```

In this example:

- The form captures the user's name and email and stores them in state variables (name and email).
- When the form is submitted, the handleSubmit() function is called, which prevents the default form submission behavior and sends a POST request to the backend using the Fetch API.
- The Content-Type: application/json header is set to indicate that the request body contains JSON data.

Handling POST Requests with Axios

The same form submission can be achieved using Axios:

```javascript
import axios from 'axios';

const handleSubmit = async (e) => {
  e.preventDefault();

  const userData = { name, email };

  try {
    const response = await
    axios.post('http://localhost:8080/api/users', userData);

    if (response.status === 201) {
      console.log('User created successfully');
    }
  } catch (error) {
    console.error('Error creating user:', error);
  }
};
```

Axios simplifies the process of sending POST requests by automatically serializing the userData object into JSON and handling the response.

Handling Form Validation

When submitting forms, it's important to validate the input to ensure that the data sent to the backend is correct. Form validation can be handled directly in React before sending the request.

```javascript
const handleSubmit = (e) => {
  e.preventDefault();

  if (!name || !email) {
    alert('Please fill in all fields');
    return;
  }

  // Send request to the backend
};
```

In this example, if the user has not entered a name or email, an alert is displayed, and the form submission is prevented.

Best Practices for Frontend-Backend Integration

Integrating React with a Spring Boot backend requires attention to detail to ensure that the application is secure, performant, and scalable. Below are some best practices to consider when connecting your frontend and backend.

1. Handling CORS (Cross-Origin Resource Sharing)

When your React frontend and Spring Boot backend are hosted on different domains or ports (e.g., localhost:3000 and localhost:8080), you may encounter **CORS** issues. CORS is a security feature implemented by browsers to restrict requests made from one domain to another.

To allow the frontend to make requests to the backend, you need to enable CORS in your Spring Boot application.

Enabling CORS in Spring Boot

```java
import org.springframework.web.bind.annotation.CrossOrigin;

@RestController
```

```
@CrossOrigin(origins = "http://localhost:3000")
public class UserController {
    // Controller methods
}
```

Alternatively, you can configure CORS globally in Spring Boot:

```java
import org.springframework.
context.annotation.Bean;
import org.springframework.web.servlet.
config.annotation.CorsRegistry;
import org.springframework.web.servlet.
config.annotation.WebMvcConfigurer;

@Bean
public WebMvcConfigurer corsConfigurer() {
    return new WebMvcConfigurer() {
        @Override
        public void addCorsMappings
(CorsRegistry registry) {
registry.addMapping("/api/**").
allowedOrigins
("http://localhost:3000");
        }
    };
}
```

2. Error Handling

Error handling is crucial when making API requests. For instance, if the backend returns an error (e.g., 404 Not Found or 500 Internal Server Error), the frontend should gracefully handle the error and provide feedback to the user.

Error Handling in Fetch

```javascript
fetch('http://localhost:8080/api/users')
  .then(response => {
    if (!response.ok) {
      throw new Error('Network response was not ok');
    }
    return response.json();
  })
  .then(data => setUsers(data))
  .catch(error => console.error('Error fetching users:', error));
```

3. Optimizing Performance

Fetching data from the backend can be slow, especially when dealing with large datasets. To improve performance, consider using **pagination** or **infinite scrolling** to load only a subset of data at a time.

Paginating Results

When fetching data from the backend, you can include pagination parameters in your request, such as page and limit:

```javascript
const fetchUsers = async (page, limit) => {
  const response = await
  fetch(`http://localhost:8080/api/users?page=${page}&limit=${limit}`);
  const data = await response.json();
  setUsers(data);
};
```

On the backend, you can implement pagination logic to return only the requested subset of data.

4. Security Best Practices

When connecting the frontend to the backend, security is paramount. Ensure that sensitive data (e.g., authentication tokens) is not exposed in the frontend code.

Using HTTPS

Always serve your application over **HTTPS** to encrypt the communication between the frontend and backend. This prevents man-in-the-middle attacks and ensures that data is securely transmitted.

Authentication and Authorization

For secure user authentication, consider implementing **JWT (JSON Web Token)**-based authentication. JWT tokens can be stored in local storage or cookies and sent with every API request to authenticate the user.

Conclusion

In this chapter, we covered how to effectively connect a React frontend with a Spring Boot backend using RESTful APIs. We explored how to fetch data, send POST requests, handle asynchronous operations, and manage global state. Additionally, we discussed best practices for integrating the frontend and backend, including error handling, CORS management, and security considerations.

With the knowledge gained in this chapter, you are well-equipped to build full-stack applications that leverage the power of React for the frontend and Spring Boot for the backend. In the next chapter, we will dive deeper into building and securing REST APIs with Spring Boot and how to create robust, production-ready backends.

Chapter 5: Building and Securing RESTful APIs with Spring Boot

RESTful APIs are a cornerstone of modern web development, providing a standardized way for different systems to communicate over the internet. In full stack development, RESTful APIs allow the frontend (built with frameworks like React) to interact with the backend (often developed using frameworks like Spring Boot) in a structured and reliable way. While creating REST APIs is crucial, ensuring they are secure and optimized for production is equally important.

In this chapter, we will explore how to build robust RESTful APIs using **Spring Boot 3**, covering topics like defining endpoints, handling HTTP requests, connecting to databases, and implementing security features like **JWT (JSON Web Tokens)** and **OAuth2**. We'll also focus on best practices for error handling, request validation, and performance optimization, ensuring your APIs are not only functional but also secure and efficient.

Introduction to RESTful API Development

As discussed in the previous chapter, **REST (Representational State Transfer)** is an architectural style that defines a set of rules and constraints for building web services. REST APIs allow the frontend and backend of an application to communicate via HTTP methods such as GET, POST, PUT, and DELETE. These methods correspond to standard CRUD (Create, Read,

Update, Delete) operations on resources such as users, products, or orders.

Core Concepts of RESTful APIs

1. **Resources**: In REST, resources are any objects that can be represented, such as users, products, or blog posts. Each resource is identified by a **URI (Uniform Resource Identifier)**. For example, a user might be accessed at /api/users/1, where 1 is the user's unique identifier.

2. **HTTP Methods**: REST uses standard HTTP methods to perform actions on resources:

- **GET**: Retrieve data from the server.
- **POST**: Create new resources.
- **PUT/PATCH**: Update existing resources.
- **DELETE**: Remove resources from the server.

1. **Statelessness**: REST APIs are stateless, meaning that each request from the client contains all the information needed to process the request. The server does not store any information about previous requests, making the system easier to scale.

2. **JSON Format**: REST APIs often use **JSON (JavaScript Object Notation)** as the data format for exchanging information between the client and the server because it is lightweight, human-readable, and easy to parse.

Creating a Basic REST API in Spring Boot 3

Spring Boot simplifies the process of creating RESTful APIs by providing built-in support for **Spring MVC** and **Spring Web**, two modules that handle web development tasks like routing, request handling, and response generation. Let's start by building a simple REST API that handles a resource called User.

Step 1: Define the User Model

First, create a simple **User** entity that represents a user resource. The User model will define the data fields that will be stored in the database.

```java
java

@Entity
public class User {
    @Id
    @GeneratedValue(strategy = GenerationType.IDENTITY)
    private Long id;

    private String name;
    private String email;

    // Getters and setters
}
```

In this example:

- The @Entity annotation marks the class as a JPA entity.
- The @Id and @GeneratedValue annotations define the id field as the primary key, which is auto-incremented.
- The name and email fields represent the user's details.

Step 2: Create the User Repository

Next, create a **UserRepository** interface that extends the **JpaRepository**. This interface provides CRUD operations without requiring any additional code.

```java
java

@Repository
public interface UserRepository extends JpaRepository<User, Long> {
}
```

The JpaRepository interface provides methods like findAll(), findById(), save(), and deleteById() out of the box, simplifying database operations.

Step 3: Create the User Service

To encapsulate the business logic, create a **UserService** class that interacts with the UserRepository.

```java
@Service
public class UserService {
    private final UserRepository userRepository;

    @Autowired
    public UserService(UserRepository userRepository) {
        this.userRepository = userRepository;
    }

    public List<User> getAllUsers() {
        return userRepository.findAll();
    }

    public User getUserById(Long id) {
        return userRepository.findById(id).orElseThrow(() -> new
        ResourceNotFoundException("User not found"));
    }

    public User createUser(User user) {
        return userRepository.save(user);
    }

    public User updateUser(Long id, User userDetails) {
        User user = userRepository.findById(id).orElseThrow(() ->
        new ResourceNotFoundException("User not found"));

        user.setName(userDetails.getName());
        user.setEmail(userDetails.getEmail());

        return userRepository.save(user);
    }

    public void deleteUser(Long id) {
        userRepository.deleteById(id);
    }
}
```

In this service:

- The getAllUsers() method retrieves all users from the database.
- The getUserById() method fetches a user by their ID, throwing an exception if the user does not exist.
- The createUser() method saves a new user to the database.
- The updateUser() method updates an existing user's details.
- The deleteUser() method removes a user from the database.

Step 4: Create the User Controller

Finally, create a **UserController** class that defines the API endpoints and maps HTTP requests to service methods.

```java
@RestController
@RequestMapping("/api/users")
public class UserController {
    private final UserService userService;

    @Autowired
    public UserController(UserService userService) {
        this.userService = userService;
    }

    @GetMapping
    public List<User> getAllUsers() {
        return userService.getAllUsers();
    }

    @GetMapping("/{id}")
    public User getUserById(@PathVariable Long id) {
        return userService.getUserById(id);
    }

    @PostMapping
    public User createUser(@RequestBody User user) {
```

```
        return userService.createUser(user);
    }

    @PutMapping("/{id}")
    public User updateUser(@PathVariable Long id, @RequestBody
    User userDetails) {
        return userService.updateUser(id, userDetails);
    }

    @DeleteMapping("/{id}")
    public void deleteUser(@PathVariable Long id) {
        userService.deleteUser(id);
    }
}
```

In this controller:

- @RestController indicates that the class is a controller that handles web requests and returns JSON responses.
- @RequestMapping("/api/users") specifies the base URL for all user-related endpoints.
- The @GetMapping, @PostMapping, @PutMapping, and @DeleteMapping annotations define the HTTP methods for interacting with the API.

With this setup, the following endpoints are available:

- GET /api/users: Retrieve all users.
- GET /api/users/{id}: Retrieve a specific user by ID.
- POST /api/users: Create a new user.
- PUT /api/users/{id}: Update an existing user.
- DELETE /api/users/{id}: Delete a user by ID.

Validating API Requests

It's crucial to validate incoming API requests to ensure that the data sent by the client is valid and conforms to your application's requirements. Spring

Boot makes it easy to validate request bodies using **Java Bean Validation** with the **Hibernate Validator**.

Step 1: Add Validation Annotations to the User Model

You can add validation constraints to the User model by annotating its fields with validation annotations such as @NotNull, @Email, and @Size.

```java
@Entity
public class User {
    @Id
    @GeneratedValue(strategy = GenerationType.IDENTITY)
    private Long id;

    @NotNull(message = "Name is required")
    @Size(min = 2, max = 50, message = "Name must be between 2 and
    50 characters")
    private String name;

    @NotNull(message = "Email is required")
    @Email(message = "Email should be valid")
    private String email;

    // Getters and setters
}
```

In this example:

- The @NotNull annotation ensures that the name and email fields are not null.
- The @Size annotation specifies the minimum and maximum length for the name field.
- The @Email annotation ensures that the email field contains a valid email address.

Step 2: Enable Validation in the Controller

To enable validation in the controller, annotate the request body parameter with @Valid.

```java
@PostMapping
public User createUser(@Valid @RequestBody User user) {
    return userService.createUser(user);
}
```

Now, when a client sends an invalid request, Spring Boot will automatically return a 400 Bad Request response with details about the validation errors.

Error Handling in REST APIs

A well-designed API should provide informative and consistent error messages when something goes wrong. Spring Boot allows you to handle errors globally by creating **exception handlers**.

Step 1: Create Custom Exceptions

Create a custom exception for resource not found errors:

```java
public class ResourceNotFoundException extends RuntimeException {
    public ResourceNotFoundException(String message) {
        super(message);
    }
}
```

Step 2: Create a Global Exception Handler

To handle exceptions globally, create a class annotated with @Controller-Advice and define methods that handle specific exceptions.

```java
@ControllerAdvice
public class GlobalExceptionHandler {
```

```
@ExceptionHandler(ResourceNotFoundException.class)
public ResponseEntity<ErrorDetails>
handleResourceNotFoundException(ResourceNotFoundException ex,
WebRequest request) {
    ErrorDetails errorDetails = new ErrorDetails(new Date(),
    ex.getMessage(), request.getDescription(false));
    return new ResponseEntity<>(errorDetails,
    HttpStatus.NOT_FOUND);
}

@ExceptionHandler(MethodArgumentNotValidException.class)
public ResponseEntity<ErrorDetails>
handleValidationExceptions(MethodArgumentNotValidException ex)
{
    String errorMessage =
    ex.getBindingResult().getFieldErrors().stream()
        .map(DefaultMessageSourceResolvable::getDefaultMessage)
        .collect(Collectors.joining(", "));
    ErrorDetails errorDetails = new ErrorDetails(new Date(),
    errorMessage, "Validation failed");
    return new ResponseEntity<>(errorDetails,
    HttpStatus.BAD_REQUEST);
}

    // Other exception handlers...
}
```

In this example:

- @ControllerAdvice marks the class as a global exception handler.
- The handleResourceNotFoundException() method handles the ResourceNotFoundException and returns a 404 Not Found response.
- The handleValidationExceptions() method handles validation errors and returns a 400 Bad Request response with the validation error messages.

Securing REST APIs with Spring Security

Security is a critical aspect of any API. **Spring Security** is a powerful framework that provides authentication, authorization, and protection against common security vulnerabilities. In this section, we'll secure the REST API using **JWT (JSON Web Token)**-based authentication and discuss additional security measures.

Step 1: Add Spring Security to the Project

To get started, add the necessary Spring Security dependencies to your pom.xml file:

xml

```xml
<dependency>
    <groupId>org.springframework.boot</groupId>
    <artifactId>spring-boot-starter-security</artifactId>
</dependency>
<dependency>
    <groupId>io.jsonwebtoken</groupId>
    <artifactId>jjwt</artifactId>
    <version>0.9.1</version>
</dependency>
```

The spring-boot-starter-security dependency includes the core Spring Security framework, while jjwt provides the tools needed to generate and verify JWT tokens.

Step 2: Configure JWT Authentication

JWT is a stateless authentication mechanism that issues a token to the client after successful login. The token is then included in every subsequent request's **Authorization** header.

1. Create a JWT Utility Class

The JWT utility class will handle the creation and validation of JWT tokens.

java

```java
@Component
public class JwtUtil {
    private String secret = "secret";
```

```java
public String generateToken(String username) {
    return Jwts.builder()
        .setSubject(username)
        .setIssuedAt(new Date(System.currentTimeMillis()))
        .setExpiration(new Date(System.currentTimeMillis() +
        1000 * 60 * 60 * 10))
        .signWith(SignatureAlgorithm.HS256, secret)
        .compact();
}

public String extractUsername(String token) {
    return Jwts.parser()
        .setSigningKey(secret)
        .parseClaimsJws(token)
        .getBody()
        .getSubject();
}

public boolean validateToken(String token, UserDetails
userDetails) {
    String username = extractUsername(token);
    return username.equals(userDetails.getUsername()) &&
    !isTokenExpired(token);
}

private boolean isTokenExpired(String token) {
    return Jwts.parser()
        .setSigningKey(secret)
        .parseClaimsJws(token)
        .getBody()
        .getExpiration()
        .before(new Date());
}
}
```

2. Create a JWT Authentication Filter

The JWT filter will intercept incoming requests and verify the JWT token.

java

```java
public class JwtRequestFilter extends OncePerRequestFilter {
    @Autowired
    private UserDetailsService userDetailsService;

    @Autowired
    private JwtUtil jwtUtil;

    @Override
    protected void doFilterInternal(HttpServletRequest request,
    HttpServletResponse response, FilterChain chain)
        throws ServletException, IOException {

        final String authorizationHeader =
        request.getHeader("Authorization");

        String username = null;
        String jwt = null;

        if (authorizationHeader != null &&
        authorizationHeader.startsWith("Bearer ")) {
            jwt = authorizationHeader.substring(7);
            username = jwtUtil.extractUsername(jwt);
        }

        if (username != null &&
        SecurityContextHolder.getContext().getAuthentication() ==
        null) {
            UserDetails userDetails =
            this.userDetailsService.loadUserByUsername(username);

            if (jwtUtil.validateToken(jwt, userDetails)) {
                UsernamePasswordAuthenticationToken
                authenticationToken = new
                UsernamePasswordAuthenticationToken(
                    userDetails, null,
                    userDetails.getAuthorities());
                authenticationToken.setDetails(new
                WebAuthenticationDetailsSource().buildDetails(request));
```

```
                    SecurityContextHolder.getContext().
setAuthentication
(authenticationToken);
            }
        }
        chain.doFilter(request, response);
    }
}
```

This filter extracts the JWT from the Authorization header, validates it, and sets the authenticated user in the security context.

3. Configure Security for the API

Finally, configure Spring Security to secure the API endpoints using JWT authentication.

```java

@Configuration
@EnableWebSecurity
public class SecurityConfig extends
WebSecurityConfigurerAdapter {

    @Autowired
    private JwtRequestFilter jwtRequestFilter;

    @Override
    protected void configure(HttpSecurity http) throws Exception {
        http.csrf().disable()
            .authorizeRequests()
            .antMatchers("/api/authenticate").permitAll()
            .anyRequest().authenticated()
            .and()
            .sessionManagement().
sessionCreationPolicy
(SessionCreationPolicy.STATELESS
```

Chapter 6: Advanced Spring Boot Features and Optimization Techniques

Building robust, scalable, and high-performance applications goes beyond basic CRUD operations and API development. As applications grow in complexity, it becomes critical to focus on architecture, performance optimization, security, and maintainability. This chapter dives into advanced features of Spring Boot that make it an excellent choice for building enterprise-grade applications. We will cover topics like microservices, caching, asynchronous programming, database optimizations, and advanced security techniques.

B y mastering these advanced features, you can create applications that are not only feature-rich but also scalable, performant, and secure, ensuring your system can handle increased load and complexity over time.

Microservices Architecture with Spring Boot

One of the significant strengths of Spring Boot is its ability to facilitate the development of **microservices**. Microservices architecture is an approach where large applications are broken down into smaller, independent services that can be deployed and scaled separately. Each microservice focuses on a specific business function, such as user management, payments, or notifications, and communicates with other microservices over the network.

Why Microservices?

Microservices offer several advantages over traditional monolithic architectures:

1. **Scalability**: Microservices can be scaled independently. If a specific part of the application (e.g., user authentication) is under heavy load, only that service can be scaled, reducing resource usage.
2. **Decoupling**: Microservices are loosely coupled, meaning changes to one service do not impact others. This promotes flexibility and easier maintenance.
3. **Independent Deployment**: Each microservice can be deployed inde-

pendently, enabling faster deployment cycles and reducing downtime.

4. **Technology Diversity**: Different microservices can use different technologies, programming languages, and databases, allowing teams to choose the best tool for the job.

Building Microservices with Spring Boot

To build microservices with Spring Boot, we need to break down our application into smaller services that can operate independently. Let's consider a system with the following microservices:

- **User Service**: Manages user registration, authentication, and user profiles.
- **Order Service**: Manages product orders, payments, and order history.
- **Notification Service**: Sends email or SMS notifications to users.

1. Creating the User Service

The **User Service** will handle user-related operations such as registration, login, and profile management. It will expose RESTful endpoints that other services can interact with.

Create a new Spring Boot project for the User Service:

```xml
Copy code
<dependency>
    <groupId>org.springframework.boot</groupId>
    <artifactId>spring-boot-starter-web</artifactId>
</dependency>
<dependency>
    <groupId>org.springframework.boot</groupId>
    <artifactId>spring-boot-starter-data-jpa</artifactId>
</dependency>
<dependency>
    <groupId>org.springframework.boot</groupId>
    <artifactId>spring-boot-starter-security</artifactId>
</dependency>
```

```
<dependency>
    <groupId>com.h2database</groupId>
    <artifactId>h2</artifactId>
</dependency>
```

The dependencies include **Spring Web** for REST APIs, **Spring Data JPA** for database interaction, **Spring Security** for securing the service, and **H2** as an in-memory database.

Example: User Service API

```java
Copy code
@RestController
@RequestMapping("/api/users")
public class UserController {

    private final UserService userService;

    @Autowired
    public UserController(UserService userService) {
        this.userService = userService;
    }

    @PostMapping("/register")
    public ResponseEntity<User> registerUser(@RequestBody User
    user) {
        User registeredUser = userService.registerUser(user);
        return new ResponseEntity<>(registeredUser,
        HttpStatus.CREATED);
    }

    @PostMapping("/login")
    public ResponseEntity<String> loginUser(@RequestBody
    UserLoginDto loginDto) {
        boolean isAuthenticated =
        userService.authenticateUser(loginDto);
        if (isAuthenticated) {
            return ResponseEntity.ok("Login successful");
```

```java
    } else {
        return
        ResponseEntity.status(HttpStatus.UNAUTHORIZED).body("Invalid
        credentials");
    }
  }
}
```

Here, the registerUser() method handles user registration, while loginUser()
processes login requests.

2. Creating the Order Service

The **Order Service** manages orders, including placing new orders, processing payments, and viewing order history. It will communicate with the
User Service to verify user credentials and process the order.

Order Service Example

```java
java
Copy code
@RestController
@RequestMapping("/api/orders")
public class OrderController {

    private final OrderService orderService;

    @Autowired
    public OrderController(OrderService orderService) {
        this.orderService = orderService;
    }

    @PostMapping
    public ResponseEntity<Order> createOrder(@RequestBody Order
    order) {
        Order newOrder = orderService.createOrder(order);
        return new ResponseEntity<>(newOrder, HttpStatus.CREATED);
    }

    @GetMapping("/{orderId}")
```

```
public ResponseEntity<Order> getOrder(@PathVariable Long
orderId) {
    Order order = orderService.getOrderById(orderId);
    return ResponseEntity.ok(order);
}
}
```

The createOrder() method handles the creation of new orders, while getOrder() retrieves an existing order by its ID.

3. Communicating Between Microservices

Microservices communicate over the network using standard protocols like HTTP or messaging systems like Kafka or RabbitMQ. In the case of HTTP-based communication, one service (e.g., Order Service) can call another service (e.g., User Service) by making an HTTP request.

To facilitate inter-service communication, Spring Boot provides **RestTemplate** and **WebClient**.

Using RestTemplate to Call Another Service

```java
Copy code
@Service
public class OrderService {

    @Autowired
    private RestTemplate restTemplate;

    public Order createOrder(Order order) {
        // Call User Service to verify user credentials
        String url = "http://localhost:8081/api/users/" +
        order.getUserId();
        ResponseEntity<User> response =
        restTemplate.getForEntity(url, User.class);

        if (response.getStatusCode() == HttpStatus.OK) {
            // Process the order
            return orderRepository.save(order);
        } else {
```

```
                throw new RuntimeException("User verification failed");
        }
    }
}
```

In this example, the **Order Service** calls the **User Service** to verify the user before processing the order. The RestTemplate class is used to send an HTTP GET request to the User Service.

Service Discovery with Eureka

In a microservices architecture, services need to be able to discover each other dynamically. Instead of hardcoding the service URLs, you can use **Eureka**, a service registry from Netflix, which allows microservices to register themselves and discover other services at runtime.

Caching for Improved Performance

As applications grow in complexity, performance optimization becomes critical. One effective way to enhance performance is by implementing **caching**. Caching involves storing frequently accessed data in memory so that subsequent requests can be served faster, reducing the load on the database.

Spring Boot provides built-in support for caching through the **Spring Cache** abstraction, which integrates with several cache providers like **Ehcache**, **Hazelcast**, and **Redis**.

Enabling Caching in Spring Boot

To enable caching in a Spring Boot application, you need to add the @EnableCaching annotation to a configuration class and annotate methods that should be cached with @Cacheable.

```java
Copy code
@Configuration
@EnableCaching
public class CacheConfig {
}
```

Using @Cacheable

The @Cacheable annotation tells Spring to cache the result of a method so that the next time the method is called with the same arguments, the cached result is returned instead of executing the method again.

```java
Copy code
@Service
public class UserService {

    @Cacheable("users")
    public User getUserById(Long id) {
        // Simulate a database call
        return userRepository.findById(id).orElseThrow(() -> new
        RuntimeException("User not found"));
    }
}
```

In this example, the getUserById() method's result is cached. When this method is called again with the same id, the cached result is returned, reducing database load.

Cache Eviction with @CacheEvict

To keep the cache consistent, you may need to evict entries from the cache when data changes. The @CacheEvict annotation removes specific cache entries.

```java
Copy code
@Service
public class UserService {

    @CacheEvict(value = "users", key = "#id")
    public void deleteUser(Long id) {
        userRepository.deleteById(id);
    }
}
```

In this example, the cache entry for the user with the given id is evicted when the user is deleted.

Choosing a Cache Provider

Spring Boot supports multiple cache providers. Some common options include:

- **Ehcache**: A popular in-memory cache provider for local caching.
- **Hazelcast**: A distributed cache provider that can be used for large-scale distributed caching.
- **Redis**: An in-memory key-value store that supports distributed caching and advanced features like persistence and replication.

To configure Redis as the cache provider, you need to add the following dependencies:

```xml
Copy code
<dependency>
    <groupId>org.springframework.boot</groupId>
    <artifactId>spring-boot-starter-data-redis</artifactId>
</dependency>
```

Then, configure Redis in the application properties:

```properties
Copy code
spring.redis.host=localhost
spring.redis.port=6379
```

Asynchronous Programming with Spring Boot

For applications that

perform I/O-bound operations like file processing, database queries, or external API calls, synchronous execution can result in bottlenecks and reduced performance. **Asynchronous programming** allows these operations to be executed concurrently, freeing up the main thread to handle other tasks while the operation completes.

Spring Boot provides support for asynchronous programming with the @Async annotation, which allows methods to run in the background.

Enabling Asynchronous Execution

To enable asynchronous execution, add the @EnableAsync annotation to a configuration class.

```java
Copy code
@Configuration
@EnableAsync
public class AsyncConfig {
}
```

Using @Async to Execute Methods Asynchronously

The @Async annotation can be applied to any method that you want to run asynchronously.

```java
Copy code
@Service
public class NotificationService {

    @Async
    public CompletableFuture<String> sendEmailNotification(String
    email) {
        // Simulate a delay in sending the email
        try {
            Thread.sleep(3000);
        } catch (InterruptedException e) {
            e.printStackTrace();
        }
        return CompletableFuture.completedFuture("Email sent to "
        + email);
    }
}
```

In this example, the sendEmailNotification() method is executed asynchronously, allowing the main thread to continue processing other requests without waiting for the email to be sent.

Returning Future or CompletableFuture

Methods annotated with @Async can return void, Future<T>, or Completab leFuture<T>. The CompletableFuture is a more powerful alternative to Future, allowing you to handle the result asynchronously and chain multiple asynchronous operations.

```java
Copy code
public CompletableFuture<String> sendEmailNotification(String
email) {
    return CompletableFuture.supplyAsync(() -> {
        // Simulate sending email
        try {
            Thread.sleep(3000);
        } catch (InterruptedException e) {
            e.printStackTrace();
        }
        return "Email sent to " + email;
    });
}
```

Optimizing Database Queries with Spring Data JPA

Efficient database interaction is crucial for the performance of any backend application. **Spring Data JPA** simplifies database access but also provides tools for optimizing queries to ensure that your application performs well under load.

1. Query Optimization with JPQL

JPQL (Java Persistence Query Language) is a powerful query language in Spring Data JPA that allows you to write custom queries. JPQL queries are translated into SQL queries that are optimized for the underlying database.

Example: Fetching users with a custom query.

```java
Copy code
```

```
@Query("SELECT u FROM User u WHERE u.name LIKE %:name%")
List<User> findUsersByName(@Param("name") String name);
```

In this example, the findUsersByName() method fetches users whose names contain the specified string.

2. Using Projections to Reduce Data Transfer

When working with large datasets, you may not need to fetch all the fields from the database. **Projections** allow you to specify which fields to retrieve, reducing the amount of data transferred from the database.

```java
Copy code
public interface UserProjection {
    String getName();
    String getEmail();
}

@Query("SELECT u.name AS name, u.email AS email FROM User u")
List<UserProjection> findUserNamesAndEmails();
```

In this example, only the name and email fields are fetched, reducing the amount of data transferred.

3. Pagination and Sorting

When querying large datasets, loading all the records at once can result in performance bottlenecks. Spring Data JPA provides built-in support for **pagination** and **sorting** to handle large datasets efficiently.

```java
Copy code
public Page<User> findAll(Pageable pageable) {
    return userRepository.findAll(pageable);
}
```

The Pageable interface allows you to specify the page size, page number, and sorting criteria.

4. Using Query Hints and Caching

Spring Data JPA allows you to use **query hints** to control the behavior of queries, such as enabling or disabling the second-level cache.

Example: Using query hints for caching.

```java
Copy code
@QueryHints(@QueryHint(name = "org.hibernate.cacheable", value =
"true"))
@Query("SELECT u FROM User u WHERE u.email = :email")
User findByEmail(@Param("email") String email);
```

In this example, the query result is cached, reducing the need to execute the same query multiple times.

Security Hardening for Production Systems

Security is a critical aspect of any enterprise application, and Spring Boot provides powerful security mechanisms to protect your system from unauthorized access, data breaches, and common attacks.

1. Securing APIs with OAuth2

OAuth2 is an industry-standard protocol for authorization. It allows users to grant third-party applications limited access to their resources without exposing their credentials.

Spring Security supports OAuth2 and allows you to configure your application to authenticate users with external identity providers like Google, Facebook, or GitHub.

To enable OAuth2 authentication, add the following dependencies to your pom.xml file:

```xml
Copy code
<dependency>
    <groupId>org.springframework.boot</groupId>
    <artifactId>spring-boot-starter-oauth2-client</artifactId>
</dependency>
```

Then, configure OAuth2 in your application.yml file:

```yaml
yaml
Copy code
spring:
  security:
    oauth2:
      client:
        registration:
          google:
            client-id: YOUR_GOOGLE_CLIENT_ID
            client-secret: YOUR_GOOGLE_CLIENT_SECRET
            scope: profile, email
            redirect-uri:
            "{baseUrl}/login/oauth2/code/{registrationId}"
```

2. Implementing Rate Limiting

To prevent abuse and denial-of-service (DoS) attacks, you can implement **rate limiting** to control the number of requests a client can make to your API within a specific time frame.

One way to implement rate limiting is by using **Bucket4j**, a Java library for rate limiting.

Add the Bucket4j dependency to your project:

```xml
xml
Copy code
<dependency>
    <groupId>com.github.vladimir-bukhtoyarov</groupId>
    <artifactId>bucket4j-core</artifactId>
    <version>7.2.0</version>
</dependency>
```

Then, configure rate limiting in a filter:

```java
java
Copy code
```

```java
@Component
public class RateLimitingFilter extends OncePerRequestFilter {

    private final Map<String, Bucket> buckets = new
    ConcurrentHashMap<>();

    @Override
    protected void doFilterInternal(HttpServletRequest request,
    HttpServletResponse response, FilterChain filterChain)
            throws ServletException, IOException {

        String clientIp = request.getRemoteAddr();
        Bucket bucket = buckets.computeIfAbsent(clientIp,
        this::newBucket);

        if (bucket.tryConsume(1)) {
            filterChain.doFilter(request, response);
        } else {
            response.setStatus(HttpStatus.TOO_MANY_REQUESTS.value());
            response.getWriter().write("Rate limit exceeded");
        }
    }

    private Bucket newBucket(String clientIp) {
        return Bucket4j.builder()
                .addLimit(Bandwidth.classic(10, Refill.greedy(10,
                Duration.ofMinutes(1))))
                .build();
    }
}
```

In this example, the **RateLimitingFilter** ensures that each client is limited to 10 requests per minute. If the client exceeds this limit, a **429 Too Many Requests** response is returned.

3. Enforcing HTTPS and Secure Headers

In production environments, it's crucial to enforce HTTPS to encrypt the communication between the client and server. Additionally, you should configure secure HTTP headers to protect against attacks like cross-site scripting (XSS), clickjacking, and content sniffing.

To enforce HTTPS, you can configure Spring Security to redirect HTTP traffic to HTTPS:

```java
Copy code
@Configuration
@EnableWebSecurity
public class SecurityConfig extends WebSecurityConfigurerAdapter {

    @Override
    protected void configure(HttpSecurity http) throws Exception {
        http.requiresChannel()
            .anyRequest()
            .requiresSecure();
    }
}
```

To set secure headers, you can use the headers() method in the Spring Security configuration:

```java
Copy code
@Override
protected void configure(HttpSecurity http) throws Exception {
    http.headers()
        .xssProtection()
        .and()
        .contentSecurityPolicy("script-src 'self'");
}
```

Conclusion

This chapter explored advanced features and optimization techniques in **Spring Boot**. We covered building microservices, caching for performance improvements, asynchronous programming for non-blocking operations, database optimization using Spring Data JPA, and implementing robust security mechanisms like OAuth2 and rate limiting.

By mastering these techniques, you can build scalable, high-performance, and secure enterprise applications with Spring Boot. In the next chapter, we'll focus on deploying your Spring Boot application to cloud platforms like AWS and managing production-level systems.

Chapter 7: Deploying Spring Boot Applications to the Cloud

Once you've built a fully functional application with Spring Boot, the next step is to deploy it so users can access it from anywhere. Cloud platforms provide scalable, reliable, and cost-effective environments to run your applications. In this chapter, we will explore how to deploy Spring Boot applications to cloud platforms like **Amazon Web Services (AWS)**, **Google Cloud Platform (GCP)**, and **Heroku**.

We will cover the essential steps for configuring your Spring Boot application for deployment, handling environment-specific configurations, setting up databases in the cloud, and ensuring the application is production-ready by implementing monitoring, logging, and scaling strategies.

Why Deploy to the Cloud?

Cloud computing has transformed the way applications are deployed and managed. Instead of managing physical servers, cloud platforms allow you to rent server space on-demand, scale your application as needed, and integrate with various cloud services for database management, storage, and networking.

Key Benefits of Cloud Deployment:

1. **Scalability**: You can easily scale up or down based on traffic and resource needs.

2. **Cost-Efficiency**: You only pay for the resources you use, reducing costs when traffic is low.
3. **High Availability**: Cloud platforms offer redundancy and failover mechanisms, ensuring your application is always accessible.
4. **Managed Services**: You can leverage managed databases, storage, monitoring tools, and more without worrying about maintaining the infrastructure.
5. **Automation**: Cloud platforms often provide built-in tools for automating deployments, updates, and scaling.

Preparing Your Spring Boot Application for Cloud Deployment

Before deploying your Spring Boot application to the cloud, it's essential to make sure it's properly configured for a cloud environment. This involves managing externalized configuration, environment variables, and security settings.

1. Externalizing Configuration

In cloud environments, you typically want to separate configuration from the code. Spring Boot provides a flexible way to externalize configuration using **application.properties** or **application.yml** files, environment variables, or command-line arguments.

Using application.yml for Environment-Specific Configurations:

You can create separate configuration files for different environments (development, staging, production). Spring Boot will automatically load the appropriate configuration based on the active profile.

```
yaml
Copy code
# application-dev.yml (Development configuration)
server:
  port: 8080
spring:
  datasource:
    url: jdbc:h2:mem:devdb
    username: sa
```

```
    password:

# application-prod.yml (Production configuration)
server:
  port: 8080
spring:
  datasource:
    url: jdbc:mysql://prod-database:3306/mydb
    username: produser
    password: prodpassword
```

In this example:

- **application-dev.yml** is used for development, where the application connects to an in-memory H2 database.
- **application-prod.yml** is used for production, where the application connects to a MySQL database hosted in the cloud.

To specify the active profile, you can use an environment variable:

```bash
bash
Copy code
java -jar myapp.jar --spring.profiles.active=prod
```

2. Managing Sensitive Information with Environment Variables

Storing sensitive information such as database credentials or API keys in your codebase is a security risk. Instead, you should use **environment variables** to store sensitive data.

Spring Boot allows you to reference environment variables directly in your configuration files:

```yaml
yaml
Copy code
```

```
spring:
  datasource:
    url: ${DB_URL}
    username: ${DB_USERNAME}
    password: ${DB_PASSWORD}
```

In this example, the DB_URL, DB_USERNAME, and DB_PASSWORD environment variables are used to configure the datasource. You can set these variables in your cloud platform's environment configuration.

3. Packaging the Application for Deployment

To deploy your Spring Boot application to the cloud, you need to package it into a **JAR (Java Archive)** or **WAR (Web Application Archive)** file. Spring Boot applications are typically packaged as executable JAR files, which can be run directly on cloud platforms.

To package the application, use the following Maven command:

```bash
Copy code
mvn clean package
```

This command creates a JAR file in the target directory that can be deployed to the cloud.

Deploying to Amazon Web Services (AWS)

Amazon Web Services (AWS) is one of the most popular cloud platforms, offering a wide range of services, including computing, storage, databases, and networking. For deploying Spring Boot applications, **Amazon EC2** (Elastic Compute Cloud) and **Elastic Beanstalk** are two commonly used services.

1. Deploying to Amazon EC2

Amazon EC2 provides virtual servers (instances) that you can configure and manage yourself. This option gives you more control over the infrastructure but requires you to handle server setup, scaling, and maintenance.

Step 1: Launch an EC2 Instance

1. Log in to your **AWS Management Console** and navigate to **EC2**.
2. Click **Launch Instance** and select the **Amazon Linux 2 AMI** as the operating system.
3. Choose an instance type (e.g., t2.micro for free-tier eligibility).
4. Configure the instance details, including networking and storage options.
5. Add security group rules to allow **HTTP** and **SSH** access.
6. Launch the instance and download the key pair (this will be used to access the instance via SSH).

Step 2: SSH into the EC2 Instance

Once the instance is running, connect to it using SSH:

```bash
Copy code
ssh -i "your-key.pem" ec2-user@your-ec2-public-ip
```

Step 3: Install Java and Upload the Spring Boot JAR

1. Install Java on the EC2 instance:

```bash
Copy code
sudo yum install java-11-amazon-corretto
```

1. Upload your Spring Boot JAR file to the EC2 instance using **SCP** (Secure Copy Protocol):

```bash
bash
Copy code
scp -i "your-key.pem" target/myapp.jar
ec2-user@your-ec2-public-ip:/home/ec2-user/
```

Step 4: Run the Spring Boot Application

Once the JAR file is uploaded, you can run the application:

```bash
bash
Copy code
java -jar myapp.jar
```

Your Spring Boot application will now be running on the EC2 instance. You can access it via the public IP of the instance.

2. Deploying to AWS Elastic Beanstalk

For a more managed deployment, **AWS Elastic Beanstalk** provides a platform-as-a-service (PaaS) that automatically handles deployment, scaling, and monitoring for you. Elastic Beanstalk simplifies the deployment process by abstracting the underlying infrastructure, allowing you to focus on your application.

Step 1: Create an Elastic Beanstalk Environment

1. Log in to the **AWS Management Console** and navigate to **Elastic Beanstalk**.
2. Click **Create New Application** and give your application a name.
3. Choose **Java** as the platform and select the platform version (e.g., Corretto 11 for Java 11).
4. Upload your Spring Boot JAR file.

Step 2: Configure the Environment

Elastic Beanstalk allows you to configure environment variables, scaling options, and load balancing. You can configure environment variables for your application (e.g., DB_URL, DB_USERNAME, and DB_PASSWORD) in the environment configuration.

Step 3: Deploy the Application

Once the environment is set up, Elastic Beanstalk will automatically deploy your application and manage the infrastructure. You can access the application using the provided **Elastic Beanstalk URL**.

Deploying to Google Cloud Platform (GCP)

Google Cloud Platform (GCP) is another popular cloud platform that provides scalable infrastructure and managed services. For deploying Spring Boot applications, **Google App Engine (GAE)** and **Google Kubernetes Engine (GKE)** are common choices.

1. Deploying to Google App Engine (GAE)

Google App Engine is a fully managed platform-as-a-service (PaaS) that allows you to deploy web applications without worrying about the underlying infrastructure. GAE automatically handles scaling, monitoring, and load balancing.

Step 1: Set Up Google Cloud SDK

1. Install the **Google Cloud SDK** by following the instructions on the Google Cloud website.
2. Authenticate your Google Cloud account:

```bash
Copy code
gcloud auth login
```

1. Set your default project:

```bash
Copy code
```

```bash
gcloud config set project your-project-id
```

Step 2: Create an App Engine Application

1. Create an App Engine application for your project:

```bash
bash
Copy code
gcloud app create
```

1. Specify the region where you want your application to be hosted.

Step 3: Configure App Engine Deployment

Create an app.yaml file in the root of your Spring Boot project to configure the deployment settings for App Engine.

```yaml
yaml
Copy code
runtime: java11
instance_class: F2
env_variables:
  SPRING_PROFILES_ACTIVE: prod
```

Step 4: Deploy the Application

To deploy your Spring Boot application to Google App Engine, use the following command:

```bash
bash
Copy code
gcloud app deploy target/myapp.jar
```

Once the deployment is complete, your application will be available on a

Google App Engine URL.

2. Deploying to Google Kubernetes Engine (GKE)

For containerized applications, **Google Kubernetes Engine (GKE)** provides a fully managed Kubernetes service that allows you to deploy, manage, and scale containerized applications.

Step 1: Containerize the Spring Boot Application

To deploy your Spring Boot

application to GKE, you need to containerize it using **Docker**.

1. Create a Dockerfile in the root of your project:

```dockerfile
Copy code
FROM openjdk:11-jre-slim
COPY target/myapp.jar myapp.jar
ENTRYPOINT ["java", "-jar", "/myapp.jar"]
```

1. Build the Docker image:

```bash
Copy code
docker build -t gcr.io/your-project-id/myapp:v1 .
```

1. Push the image to **Google Container Registry (GCR)**:

```bash
Copy code
docker push gcr.io/your-project-id/myapp:v1
```

Step 2: Set Up a Kubernetes Cluster

1. Create a Kubernetes cluster on GKE:

```bash
Copy code
gcloud container clusters create my-cl
```

Chapter 8: Monitoring, Logging, and Scaling Spring Boot Applications

Once your Spring Boot application is deployed to the cloud, it becomes crucial to ensure that the application performs optimally, remains reliable under high traffic, and is easy to troubleshoot when issues arise. Monitoring, logging, and scaling are essential practices that help maintain the health of the application, track performance, and ensure that resources are used efficiently.

I n this chapter, we will explore best practices for monitoring, logging, and scaling Spring Boot applications. We'll cover the various tools and techniques available for collecting performance metrics, logging application behavior, automating scaling processes, and troubleshooting common issues in production environments.

The Importance of Monitoring and Logging

Monitoring and logging are essential components of managing a production application. They provide visibility into how the application is performing, help identify potential issues before they escalate, and facilitate quick diagnosis when problems occur.

Why Monitoring Matters

Monitoring ensures that the application is running as expected by tracking key performance indicators (KPIs) such as CPU usage, memory consumption, response times, and error rates. Without proper monitoring, it can be difficult to detect issues like performance bottlenecks, resource exhaustion, or system failures.

Why Logging Matters

Logging allows you to capture detailed information about the application's behavior. Logs record events such as user actions, errors, warnings, and system activities, providing valuable insight into what's happening inside the application. Logs are essential for diagnosing issues, auditing activities, and understanding how the application is used.

Monitoring Spring Boot Applications

Spring Boot provides built-in support for application monitoring through the **Spring Boot Actuator** module. Actuator exposes endpoints that provide insights into the health and performance of your application, including metrics on memory usage, CPU load, HTTP requests, and database connections.

1. Enabling Spring Boot Actuator

To enable Actuator in your Spring Boot application, add the following dependency to your pom.xml file:

```xml
Copy code
<dependency>
    <groupId>org.springframework.boot</groupId>
    <artifactId>spring-boot-starter-actuator</artifactId>
</dependency>
```

After adding the dependency, Actuator will expose several monitoring endpoints by default. You can view available endpoints at /actuator.

2. Exposing Actuator Endpoints

You can configure which Actuator endpoints are exposed in the application.yml or application.properties file. By default, most endpoints are disabled or restricted for security reasons, but you can enable specific endpoints based on your needs.

```yaml
Copy code
management:
  endpoints:
    web:
      exposure:
        include: health, info, metrics, prometheus
```

The above configuration exposes the **health**, **info**, **metrics**, and **prometheus** endpoints, which provide important information about the application's status and performance.

3. Key Actuator Endpoints

- **/actuator/health**: Provides the health status of the application (e.g., UP or DOWN). You can extend this endpoint to include custom health checks for your database, messaging systems, or other components.
- **/actuator/info**: Displays general information about the application, such as version number and build information.
- **/actuator/metrics**: Provides detailed metrics on system performance, such as memory usage, CPU load, and active threads. You can also access specific metrics (e.g., /actuator/metrics/jvm.memory.used).
- **/actuator/prometheus**: Exposes metrics in a format compatible with **Prometheus**, a popular monitoring and alerting toolkit. This endpoint is useful for integrating with external monitoring systems.

4. Custom Health Checks

You can add custom health checks to the /actuator/health endpoint by implementing the HealthIndicator interface. This allows you to monitor the health of specific components of your application.

```java
Copy code
@Component
public class DatabaseHealthIndicator implements HealthIndicator {

    @Autowired
    private DataSource dataSource;

    @Override
    public Health health() {
        try (Connection connection = dataSource.getConnection()) {
            if (connection.isValid(1)) {
                return Health.up().withDetail("Database",
                "Available").build();
            }
        } catch (SQLException e) {
            return Health.down().withDetail("Database", "Not
            Available").build();
        }
```

```
        return Health.unknown().build();
    }
}
```

In this example, a custom health check is created for the database connection. The health check returns **UP** if the database is available and **DOWN** if it is not.

Using Prometheus and Grafana for Monitoring

Prometheus and **Grafana** are powerful open-source tools that are commonly used for monitoring and visualization in production environments. Prometheus collects metrics from your application, while Grafana provides a dashboard for visualizing those metrics in real-time.

1. Setting Up Prometheus

To monitor your Spring Boot application with Prometheus, you need to configure Prometheus to scrape metrics from the /actuator/prometheus endpoint.

Step 1: Install Prometheus

Download and install Prometheus from the official Prometheus website.

Step 2: Configure Prometheus

Create a prometheus.yml configuration file to specify the targets that Prometheus should monitor. Add your Spring Boot application's /actuator/prometheus endpoint as a target.

```yaml
Copy code
scrape_configs:
  - job_name: 'spring-boot-app'
    static_configs:
      - targets: ['localhost:8080'] # Replace with your
      application's host and port
```

Step 3: Start Prometheus

Run Prometheus using the following command:

```bash
Copy code
./prometheus --config.file=prometheus.yml
```

Prometheus will now scrape metrics from your Spring Boot application.

2. Setting Up Grafana

Grafana is a visualization tool that integrates with Prometheus to display metrics on interactive dashboards.

Step 1: Install Grafana

Download and install Grafana from the official Grafana website.

Step 2: Add Prometheus as a Data Source

Once Grafana is running, log in to the Grafana dashboard, navigate to **Configuration > Data Sources**, and add Prometheus as a data source. Provide the URL of your Prometheus server (e.g., http://localhost:9090).

Step 3: Create Dashboards

You can create custom dashboards to visualize metrics such as memory usage, request latency, and error rates. Grafana provides a range of pre-built dashboards for Spring Boot applications, which you can import from the **Grafana Dashboards** library.

Logging in Spring Boot Applications

Effective logging is essential for debugging, troubleshooting, and auditing your application. Spring Boot provides out-of-the-box logging using **Logback**, but it also integrates with other logging frameworks like **Log4j** and **SLF4J**.

1. Configuring Logback in Spring Boot

Spring Boot uses **Logback** as the default logging framework. You can configure Logback by creating a logback-spring.xml file in the src/main/resources directory.

```xml
Copy code
<configuration>
    <appender name="CONSOLE"
```

```
        class="ch.qos.logback.core.ConsoleAppender">
            <encoder>
                <pattern>%d{yyyy-MM-dd HH:mm:ss} - %msg%n</pattern>
            </encoder>
        </appender>

        <root level="INFO">
            <appender-ref ref="CONSOLE" />
        </root>
    </configuration>
```

In this example, logs are printed to the console, and the log level is set to INFO. You can adjust the log level to DEBUG, WARN, or ERROR based on your needs.

2. Logging Best Practices

To ensure that your logs provide meaningful information, follow these best practices:

- **Use log levels appropriately**: Log levels should reflect the severity of the message. For example, use DEBUG for development details, INFO for general information, WARN for potential issues, and ERROR for critical errors.
- **Include contextual information**: Include useful information in log messages, such as request IDs, user IDs, or transaction IDs, to make it easier to trace specific events.
- **Log exceptions**: When logging exceptions, include the stack trace to provide insight into the source of the error.

3. Centralized Logging with ELK Stack

In production environments, it's common to use centralized logging systems to aggregate logs from multiple instances of the application. The **ELK Stack** (Elasticsearch, Logstash, and Kibana) is a popular solution for centralized logging.

Step 1: Install Elasticsearch and Logstash

Elasticsearch is a distributed search and analytics engine, and Logstash is a data processing pipeline that collects, parses, and stores logs in Elasticsearch.

Download and install Elasticsearch and Logstash from the Elasticsearch website.

Step 2: Configure Logstash to Collect Logs

Create a Logstash configuration file that specifies how to collect and process logs from your Spring Boot application.

```bash
Copy code
input {
    file {
        path => "/var/log/spring-boot-app/*.log"
        start_position => "beginning"
    }
}

output {
    elasticsearch {
        hosts => ["localhost:9200"]
        index => "spring-boot-logs"
    }
}
```

This configuration collects logs from the specified file path and sends them to Elasticsearch.

Step 3: Visualize Logs in Kibana

Install Kibana, a data visualization tool that works with Elasticsearch. Kibana allows you to create dashboards for analyzing logs and identifying patterns.

Once Kibana is running, log in to the Kibana dashboard and configure an index

pattern to visualize the logs stored in Elasticsearch.

Scaling Spring Boot Applications

Scaling ensures that your application can handle increased load by adding resources as needed. Scaling can be achieved vertically (adding more power to an existing server) or horizontally (adding more instances).

1. Vertical Scaling

Vertical scaling involves increasing the resources of the existing server, such as CPU, memory, or storage. This is often the simplest scaling approach but has limitations due to hardware constraints. Vertical scaling is ideal for small applications or temporary spikes in demand.

2. Horizontal Scaling

Horizontal scaling involves adding more instances of the application to distribute the load. Horizontal scaling is more flexible and is the preferred method for handling increased traffic in modern applications.

Scaling with Load Balancers

A **load balancer** distributes incoming traffic across multiple instances of the application, ensuring that no single instance is overwhelmed. Load balancing also provides fault tolerance by automatically rerouting traffic in case an instance becomes unavailable.

AWS Elastic Load Balancer (ELB), **Google Cloud Load Balancer**, and **Nginx** are popular load balancing solutions.

Auto Scaling

Auto scaling automatically adjusts the number of instances based on the current load. Most cloud platforms offer auto scaling features, allowing you to define policies for scaling up or down based on metrics like CPU usage or network traffic.

For example, **AWS Auto Scaling** can automatically launch new EC2 instances when CPU usage exceeds a defined threshold and terminate instances when usage drops.

3. Scaling with Kubernetes

Kubernetes is a powerful container orchestration platform that simplifies the deployment, scaling, and management of containerized applications. Kubernetes automates scaling by monitoring resource utilization and adding or removing containers as needed.

Kubernetes Horizontal Pod Autoscaler

The **Horizontal Pod Autoscaler (HPA)** is a feature in Kubernetes that automatically scales the number of pods in a deployment based on CPU or memory usage.

To enable HPA, you can define a configuration that specifies the target CPU utilization for the application.

```yaml
Copy code
apiVersion: autoscaling/v1
kind: HorizontalPodAutoscaler
metadata:
  name: spring-boot-app-hpa
spec:
  scaleTargetRef:
    apiVersion: apps/v1
    kind: Deployment
    name: spring-boot-app
  minReplicas: 2
  maxReplicas: 10
  targetCPUUtilizationPercentage: 80
```

In this example, Kubernetes will maintain between 2 and 10 replicas of the spring-boot-app deployment, scaling up or down based on CPU utilization.

Handling Common Production Issues

Running a Spring Boot application in production can come with challenges such as high memory usage, slow response times, and unexpected crashes. Below are some strategies for diagnosing and resolving common production issues.

1. High Memory Usage

If your application is experiencing high memory usage, it could lead to **OutOfMemoryError** crashes. You can use the following strategies to diagnose and resolve memory issues:

- **Heap Dumps**: Generate a heap dump to analyze memory usage and identify objects consuming excessive memory.
- **Garbage Collection Logs**: Enable garbage collection (GC) logging to analyze the frequency and duration of GC events.
- **Use a Memory Profiler**: Tools like **VisualVM** or **JProfiler** can help

you analyze memory usage and identify memory leaks.

2. Slow Response Times

Slow response times can be caused by high CPU usage, slow database queries, or resource contention. To identify the root cause, you can use:

- **Thread Dumps**: Generate a thread dump to analyze the state of threads in your application and identify bottlenecks.
- **APM Tools**: **Application Performance Monitoring (APM)** tools like **New Relic**, **AppDynamics**, or **Datadog** provide deep insights into application performance, including request latency and slow transactions.

3. Unexpected Application Crashes

Unexpected crashes can occur due to unhandled exceptions, resource exhaustion, or configuration errors. To troubleshoot crashes:

- **Analyze Logs**: Review logs to identify error messages and stack traces leading up to the crash.
- **Monitor Metrics**: Use monitoring tools like Prometheus and Grafana to check for resource exhaustion (e.g., high CPU or memory usage) before the crash occurred.
- **Configure Alerts**: Set up alerts for key metrics like CPU usage, memory consumption, and error rates to be notified before the application crashes.

Conclusion

In this chapter, we explored essential practices for monitoring, logging, and scaling Spring Boot applications in production. We discussed using **Spring Boot Actuator** to expose monitoring endpoints, integrating with **Prometheus** and **Grafana** for visualization, and implementing effective logging strategies with **Logback** and the **ELK Stack**.

We also covered scaling strategies, including vertical and horizontal scaling, load balancing, and using **Kubernetes** for container orchestration. Finally, we discussed how to handle common production issues such as high memory usage, slow response times, and unexpected crashes.

By implementing these best practices, you can ensure that your Spring Boot application remains reliable, performant, and easy to manage, even under heavy load. In the next chapter, we will focus on optimizing database performance and handling transactions efficiently using Spring Data and JPA.

Chapter 9: Optimizing Database Performance and Handling Transactions with Spring Data JPA

A well-designed database is critical for any full-stack application. When building backend systems, especially those handling large volumes of data, optimizing database performance becomes a priority. Spring Data JPA (Java Persistence API) provides an abstraction over databases, making it easier to interact with relational databases while handling CRUD operations, queries, and transactions. However, to ensure the best performance and efficiency, certain optimization techniques and transaction management strategies are necessary.

I n this chapter, we'll explore key database optimization strategies, advanced query techniques, transaction management with Spring Data JPA, and how to avoid common pitfalls like n+1 queries, inefficient joins, and database locking issues. We will also cover the best practices for working with relational databases in Spring Boot, caching strategies, and database profiling.

Why Database Optimization Matters

Before diving into the technical details, it's important to understand why database optimization is crucial for any application:

1. **Performance**: Optimizing database interactions ensures faster query execution, reducing latency and improving the user experience.
2. **Scalability**: A well-optimized database can handle more users and larger datasets without slowing down or crashing.
3. **Cost-Efficiency**: Optimized databases make efficient use of resources, reducing the cost of hardware and cloud resources.
4. **Stability**: Reducing database bottlenecks minimizes the risk of system crashes, data corruption, or transaction deadlocks.

Understanding Spring Data JPA and Its Features

Spring Data JPA is built on top of **Hibernate**, a popular ORM (Object-Relational Mapping) framework, and abstracts many of the complexities of interacting with databases. It simplifies common database tasks such as

CRUD operations, query generation, pagination, and transaction management.

Key Features of Spring Data JPA:

- **Repository Abstraction**: Provides a set of repository interfaces for common database operations, such as saving, finding, and deleting entities.
- **JPQL (Java Persistence Query Language)**: Allows writing custom queries in an object-oriented form that Hibernate translates into SQL.
- **Criteria API**: Enables dynamic query generation in a type-safe manner.
- **Transaction Management**: Built-in support for managing database transactions, allowing for atomic operations.
- **Pagination and Sorting**: Supports paginated queries to retrieve large datasets efficiently and avoid overloading the application with too much data at once.

Optimizing Database Interactions in Spring Data JPA

The way you interact with the database has a direct impact on performance. By leveraging the features of Spring Data JPA, you can ensure your application is making efficient use of the database.

1. Use Proper Indexing

Indexes significantly improve the performance of queries by allowing the database to locate rows more quickly. Without indexes, the database must perform a full table scan to retrieve results, which is time-consuming, especially for large tables.

Creating Indexes in a Relational Database

Most relational databases allow you to create indexes on one or more columns. For example, in MySQL, you can create an index on the email column of a User table:

```
sql
Copy code
```

```
CREATE INDEX idx_user_email ON User (email);
```

Indexes are particularly useful for:

- **Columns used in WHERE clauses.**
- **Columns used in JOIN operations.**
- **Columns that are frequently searched or sorted.**

Be mindful of over-indexing, as creating too many indexes can negatively impact performance during write operations (INSERT, UPDATE, DELETE).

2. Avoid the N+1 Query Problem

The **N+1 query problem** occurs when the application performs a query to retrieve a list of entities (N), and then for each entity, it executes another query to fetch related data. This results in N+1 queries being executed instead of just two or three queries.

Example of N+1 Problem

Let's consider an example where you fetch a list of users, and for each user, you also want to retrieve their associated posts.

```java
Copy code
// N+1 problem
List<User> users = userRepository.findAll();
for (User user : users) {
    List<Post> posts = postRepository.findByUserId(user.getId());
}
```

Here, the application executes one query to fetch all users and then one additional query for each user to fetch their posts, resulting in N+1 queries.

Solution: Using JOIN FETCH

You can eliminate the N+1 problem by using the **JOIN FETCH** keyword in your JPQL queries, which allows you to fetch related entities in a single query.

```java
Copy code
@Query("SELECT u FROM User u JOIN FETCH u.posts")
List<User> findAllUsersWithPosts();
```

In this example, a single query fetches both users and their associated posts, avoiding the N+1 problem.

3. Leverage Pagination for Large Result Sets

Retrieving large datasets all at once can overwhelm both the application and the database, leading to performance bottlenecks. Instead, you should use pagination to retrieve data in smaller chunks.

Spring Data JPA provides built-in support for pagination through the Pageable interface, which allows you to fetch results page by page.

Example of Pagination with Spring Data JPA

```java
Copy code
Page<User> findAll(Pageable pageable);
```

To retrieve a paginated list of users, you can specify the page size and page number:

```java
Copy code
Pageable pageable = PageRequest.of(0, 20); // Page 0, 20 records
per page
Page<User> usersPage = userRepository.findAll(pageable);
```

Using pagination ensures that your application can handle large datasets without consuming too much memory or slowing down the database.

4. Write Efficient Queries with JPQL

While Spring Data JPA generates queries automatically for simple CRUD operations, you may need to write custom queries for more complex use cases. JPQL allows you to write queries that are optimized for your specific needs.

Example of a JPQL Query

```java
Copy code
@Query("SELECT u FROM User u WHERE u.age > :age ORDER BY u.name")
List<User> findUsersOlderThan(@Param("age") int age);
```

JPQL provides a powerful way to write complex queries, including:

- **Joins**: Combining data from multiple tables.
- **Subqueries**: Nesting queries to retrieve more specific data.
- **Aggregation Functions**: Using functions like COUNT(), AVG(), and SUM() to calculate values.

5. Use Projections to Reduce Data Transfer

When you don't need all fields from a database entity, you can use **projections** to retrieve only the necessary fields. This reduces the amount of data transferred between the database and your application, improving performance.

Example of Projections

```java
Copy code
public interface UserProjection {
    String getName();
    String getEmail();
}
```

```java
@Query("SELECT u.name AS name, u.email AS email FROM User u")
List<UserProjection> findUserNamesAndEmails();
```

In this example, only the name and email fields are retrieved, reducing the data transferred from the database to the application.

6. Use Batch Processing for Bulk Operations

When performing bulk operations (e.g., inserting or updating many rows), it's more efficient to use **batch processing** to reduce the number of database round-trips.

Spring Data JPA supports batch processing for operations like saving multiple entities at once.

Example of Batch Insert

```java
Copy code
@Modifying
@Query("INSERT INTO User (name, email) VALUES (:name, :email)")
void batchInsert(@Param("name") String name, @Param("email")
String email);
```

You can configure Spring Boot to enable batch processing by setting the following property in application.yml:

```yaml
Copy code
spring:
  jpa:
    properties:
      hibernate.jdbc.batch_size: 20
```

This configuration ensures that insert or update operations are batched into groups of 20 before being sent to the database, reducing the number of network round-trips and improving performance.

Managing Transactions with Spring Data JPA

Database transactions are an essential part of any application that involves data modifications. A transaction ensures that a series of operations are treated as a single unit of work. If any part of the transaction fails, all operations are rolled back to maintain data consistency.

1. Understanding ACID Properties

Transactions are governed by **ACID (Atomicity, Consistency, Isolation, Durability)** properties:

- **Atomicity**: Ensures that all operations in a transaction succeed or none do.
- **Consistency**: Ensures that the database moves from one valid state to another after the transaction.
- **Isolation**: Ensures that transactions are executed in isolation and do not interfere with each other.
- **Durability**: Ensures that once a transaction is committed, the changes are permanently saved, even in the event of a system crash.

2. Enabling Transaction Management

Spring Data JPA provides built-in support for managing transactions using the @Transactional annotation. This annotation can be applied to methods or classes to ensure that all database operations within the method are wrapped in a transaction.

Example of @Transactional

```java
Copy code
@Service
public class UserService {

    @Transactional
    public void createUser(User user) {
        userRepository.save(user);
        // Additional database operations...
    }
}
```

In this example, if any operation within the createUser() method fails, all changes made to the database are rolled back.

3. Controlling Transaction Propagation

Transaction propagation defines how transactions should behave when one transaction calls another method that is also transactional. Spring Data JPA supports several propagation behaviors, including:

- **REQUIRED**: The default propagation behavior. If a transaction already exists, the method joins that transaction; otherwise,

Chapter 10: Building RESTful APIs with Spring Boot and React

In a full-stack development environment, building seamless communication between the frontend and backend is crucial. With Spring Boot managing the backend and React handling the frontend, the two can communicate effectively through RESTful APIs. REST APIs provide a standardized way for the frontend to request data from the backend and send data back to it. In this chapter, we will dive deeper into building RESTful APIs with Spring Boot and consuming them with React, covering best practices, error handling, security, and how to ensure smooth communication between both parts of the stack.

By the end of this chapter, you will understand how to create, secure, and optimize RESTful APIs in Spring Boot and how to fetch and send data from React using libraries like **Axios** or the native **Fetch API**.

Introduction to RESTful API Design

A **RESTful API** (Representational State Transfer) is a type of web service that allows a client (e.g., a React app) to interact with a server (e.g., a Spring Boot app) using standard HTTP methods like **GET**, **POST**, **PUT**, and **DELETE**. Each HTTP method corresponds to a different type of operation:

- **GET**: Retrieve data from the server.
- **POST**: Send data to the server to create a new resource.
- **PUT**: Update an existing resource.
- **DELETE**: Remove a resource from the server.

A well-designed RESTful API adheres to the principles of **statelessness**, **uniform interfaces**, and **resource-based URLs**.

Statelessness

RESTful APIs are stateless, meaning that each request from the client must contain all the information needed to fulfill the request. The server does not store any session information between requests.

Uniform Interface

APIs should have a consistent interface where resources are identified by URIs (Uniform Resource Identifiers). For example, a user resource might be represented by /api/users, and an individual user could be accessed via /api/users/{id}.

HTTP Methods and Status Codes

Using the appropriate HTTP method is key to maintaining a clean API design:

- **GET**: Used to retrieve data.
- **POST**: Used to create a new resource.
- **PUT/PATCH**: Used to update an existing resource.
- **DELETE**: Used to delete a resource.

Each HTTP response from the API should include an appropriate status code to indicate the outcome of the request:

- **200 OK**: The request was successful.
- **201 Created**: A new resource was successfully created.
- **400 Bad Request**: The request was invalid or cannot be processed.
- **401 Unauthorized**: The client is not authenticated to access the resource.
- **404 Not Found**: The requested resource could not be found.
- **500 Internal Server Error**: There was an error on the server.

Building RESTful APIs in Spring Boot

Spring Boot makes it easy to build RESTful APIs by providing built-in tools for routing, request handling, and response generation. In this section, we will create a simple API for managing users in a system, covering CRUD (Create, Read, Update, Delete) operations.

Step 1: Setting Up the Spring Boot Project

Start by setting up a basic Spring Boot project. Use Maven or Gradle to include the necessary dependencies, such as **Spring Web**, **Spring Data JPA**, and **H2** for the in-memory database.

```xml
xml
Copy code
<dependencies>
    <dependency>
        <groupId>org.springframework.boot</groupId>
        <artifactId>spring-boot-starter-web</artifactId>
    </dependency>
    <dependency>
        <groupId>org.springframework.boot</groupId>
        <artifactId>spring-boot-starter-data-jpa</artifactId>
    </dependency>
    <dependency>
        <groupId>com.h2database</groupId>
        <artifactId>h2</artifactId>
        <scope>runtime</scope>
    </dependency>
</dependencies>
```

Step 2: Creating the User Model

The user model represents a typical user in our system, with fields like id, name, and email. Using **JPA annotations**, we can map this model to a database table.

```java
java
Copy code
@Entity
public class User {

    @Id
    @GeneratedValue(strategy = GenerationType.IDENTITY)
    private Long id;

    private String name;
    private String email;

    // Getters and setters
}
```

Step 3: Creating the User Repository

Spring Data JPA provides repository interfaces for database interactions. The UserRepository interface extends JpaRepository, allowing us to perform CRUD operations without writing any SQL queries.

```java
Copy code
@Repository
public interface UserRepository extends JpaRepository<User, Long> {
}
```

Step 4: Building the User Service

The UserService class will handle business logic, providing methods to retrieve, create, update, and delete users.

```java
Copy code
@Service
public class UserService {

    @Autowired
    private UserRepository userRepository;

    public List<User> getAllUsers() {
        return userRepository.findAll();
    }

    public User getUserById(Long id) {
        return userRepository.findById(id)
                .orElseThrow(() -> new
                ResourceNotFoundException("User not found"));
    }

    public User createUser(User user) {
        return userRepository.save(user);
    }

    public User updateUser(Long id, User userDetails) {
```

```
    User user = getUserById(id);
    user.setName(userDetails.getName());
    user.setEmail(userDetails.getEmail());
    return userRepository.save(user);
}

public void deleteUser(Long id) {
    userRepository.deleteById(id);
}
}
```

Step 5: Creating the User Controller

The UserController class handles HTTP requests and routes them to the appropriate service methods. Each method corresponds to a specific HTTP operation (GET, POST, PUT, DELETE).

```java
Copy code
@RestController
@RequestMapping("/api/users")
public class UserController {

    @Autowired
    private UserService userService;

    @GetMapping
    public List<User> getAllUsers() {
        return userService.getAllUsers();
    }

    @GetMapping("/{id}")
    public User getUserById(@PathVariable Long id) {
        return userService.getUserById(id);
    }

    @PostMapping
    public User createUser(@RequestBody User user) {
```

```java
        return userService.createUser(user);
    }

    @PutMapping("/{id}")
    public User updateUser(@PathVariable Long id, @RequestBody
    User user) {
        return userService.updateUser(id, user);
    }

    @DeleteMapping("/{id}")
    public void deleteUser(@PathVariable Long id) {
        userService.deleteUser(id);
    }
}
```

This setup creates a fully functional RESTful API for managing users. You can now retrieve, create, update, and delete users via HTTP requests.

Consuming RESTful APIs in React

On the frontend, **React** is responsible for making requests to the Spring Boot API and displaying the data to users. In this section, we'll explore how to fetch data from a Spring Boot API, handle form submissions, and manage the application state in React.

1. Fetching Data with Axios

Axios is a popular HTTP client for making API requests in JavaScript. It simplifies the process of sending requests and handling responses.

To install Axios, use the following command:

```bash
bash
Copy code
npm install axios
```

Fetching Data from the API

In React, you can use the useEffect hook to fetch data when the component mounts. Axios can be used to send a **GET** request to the Spring Boot API.

```javascript
javascript
Copy code
import React, { useEffect, useState } from 'react';
import axios from 'axios';

const UserList = () => {
    const [users, setUsers] = useState([]);

    useEffect(() => {
        axios.get('/api/users')
            .then(response => {
                setUsers(response.data);
            })
            .catch(error => {
                console.error('Error fetching users:', error);
            });
    }, []);

    return (
        <div>
            <h1>User List</h1>
            <ul>
                {users.map(user => (
                    <li key={user.id}>{user.name} -
                    {user.email}</li>
                ))}
            </ul>
        </div>
    );
};

export default UserList;
```

In this example:

- The **GET** request is made to the /api/users endpoint to retrieve a list of users.
- The response data is stored in the users state variable, which is then displayed in a list.

2. Handling Form Submissions

To send data to the backend, you can use a form in React and handle the submission with Axios. For example, to create a new user, you can use a **POST** request.

```javascript
Copy code
import React, { useState } from 'react';
import axios from 'axios';

const CreateUser = () => {
    const [name, setName] = useState('');
    const [email, setEmail] = useState('');

    const handleSubmit = (e) => {
        e.preventDefault();
        const user = { name, email };

        axios.post('/api/users', user)
            .then(response => {
                console.log('User created:', response.data);
            })
            .catch(error => {
                console.error('Error creating user:', error);
            });
    };

    return (
        <div>
            <h1>Create User</h1>
            <form onSubmit={handleSubmit}>
                <div>
                    <label>Name:</
```

label> <input type="text" value={name} onChange={(e) => setName(e.target.value)} /> </div> <div> <label>Email:</label> <input type="email" value={email} onChange={(e) => setEmail(e.target.value)} /> </div> <button type="submit">Create User</button> </form> </div>); };

export default CreateUser;

```sql
Copy code
```

In this example:
- The user's name and email are captured in form inputs.
- When the form is submitted, a **POST** request is sent to
`/api/users` with the user's details.

Chapter 11: Implementing Security for Full Stack Applications

I n any modern full stack application, security is a primary concern. When building a full stack project using **Spring Boot** for the backend and **React** for the frontend, it's critical to ensure secure communication between both sides, protect sensitive information, and implement authentication and authorization mechanisms effectively. In this chapter, we will focus on securing your application by implementing best practices for authentication, using **JWT (JSON Web Token)** for stateless sessions, and managing authorization to protect resources from unauthorized access.

The Basics of Web Application Security

Web application security focuses on protecting the application from malicious activities, unauthorized access, data breaches, and vulnerabilities. When implementing security in a full stack application, you should consider the following layers:

- **Authentication**: Verifying the identity of the user trying to access the system.
- **Authorization**: Determining the permissions of an authenticated user— what actions they can perform and what resources they can access.
- **Data Encryption**: Protecting data transmitted between the client and

the server using encryption.

- **Input Validation**: Ensuring that the data received from the user is clean and safe to prevent attacks like SQL injection or XSS.

Authentication and Authorization with Spring Security

Spring Security is a powerful and customizable framework that provides authentication, authorization, and protection against common security vulnerabilities. It integrates seamlessly with Spring Boot and can be customized to fit the security requirements of your application.

1. Setting Up Spring Security

To secure your Spring Boot application, start by adding the **Spring Security** dependency to your pom.xml:

```xml
Copy code
<dependency>
    <groupId>org.springframework.boot</groupId>
    <artifactId>spring-boot-
starter-security</artifactId>
</dependency>
```

By default, Spring Security adds basic authentication to all endpoints, requiring a username and password for every request. While this can be a useful starting point, a more robust and user-friendly approach involves using **JWT (JSON Web Tokens)** for authentication and session management.

2. Authentication Using JWT

JWT (JSON Web Token) is a widely used standard for stateless authentication in modern web applications. It allows the server to issue a token to the client after successful authentication, which the client includes in subsequent requests to verify their identity.

Step 1: Configure UserDetailsService and JWT Utility

First, define a custom **UserDetailsService** to load user details during authentication:

```java
Copy code
@Service
public class CustomUserDetailsService
 implements UserDetailsService {

    @Autowired
    private UserRepository userRepository;

    @Override
    public UserDetails loadUserByUsername
(String username) throws
UsernameNotFoundException {
        User user = userRepository.
findByUsername(username)
                .orElseThrow(() -> new UsernameNotFoundException
("User not found"));
        return new org.springframework.
security.core.userdetails.
User(user.getUsername(),
user.getPassword(),
                new ArrayList<>());
    }
}
```

Next, create a **JwtUtil** class to handle the generation and validation of JWT
tokens:

```java
Copy code
@Component
public class JwtUtil {
    private String secret =
"secretKey"; // Use a secure,
environment-specific key in production

    public String generateToken
(String username) {
```

```
        return Jwts.builder()
                .setSubject(username)
.setIssuedAt(new Date(System.
currentTimeMillis()))
                .setExpiration(new Date
(System.currentTimeMillis() +
 1000 * 60 * 60 * 10)) //
Token valid for 10 hours
                .signWith
(SignatureAlgorithm.HS256, secret)
                .compact();
    }

    public String extractUsername
(String token) {
        return Jwts.parser().
setSigningKey(secret).
parseClaimsJws(token).
getBody().getSubject();
    }

    public boolean validateToken
(String token, UserDetails userDetails) {
        String username =
extractUsername(token);
        return username.equals
(userDetails.getUsername()) &&
!isTokenExpired(token);
    }

    private boolean isTokenExpired
(String token) {
        return Jwts.parser().
setSigningKey(secret).
parseClaimsJws(token).getBody().
getExpiration().before(new Date());
    }
}
```

Step 2: Create an Authentication Controller

Create a controller to handle user login and generate the JWT token:

```java
Copy code
@RestController
@RequestMapping("/api/auth")
public class AuthController {

    @Autowired
    private AuthenticationManager
 authenticationManager;

    @Autowired
    private CustomUserDetailsService
 userDetailsService;

    @Autowired
    private JwtUtil jwtUtil;

    @PostMapping("/login")
    public ResponseEntity<?>
login(@RequestBody
AuthRequest authRequest) {
        try {
authenticationManager.authenticate(
                new UsernamePassword
AuthenticationToken(
authRequest.getUsername(),
authRequest.getPassword())
            );
        } catch (BadCredentialsException e) {
            return ResponseEntity.
status(HttpStatus.
UNAUTHORIZED).body("Invalid credentials");
        }

        UserDetails userDetails =
        userDetailsService.loadUserByUsername
(authRequest.getUsername());
        String jwtToken = jwtUtil.generateToken
```

```
userDetails.getUsername());

        return ResponseEntity.ok
(new AuthResponse(jwtToken));
    }
}
```

The login() method authenticates the user using the provided credentials. If authentication is successful, a JWT token is generated and returned to the client.

Step 3: Secure Endpoints with JWT Authentication

Configure a filter to intercept incoming requests and validate the JWT token:

```java
java
Copy code
public class JwtRequest
Filter extends O
ncePerRequestFilter {

    @Autowired
    private JwtUtil jwtUtil;

    @Autowired
    private CustomUserDetailsService
 userDetailsService;

    @Override
    protected void doFilterInternal
(HttpServletRequest request,
HttpServletResponse response,
 FilterChain chain)
throws ServletException, IOException {

        String authorizationHeader =
        request.getHeader("Authorization");

        String username = null;
```

```
        String jwt = null;

if (authorizationHeader != null &&
authorizationHeader.startsWith("Bearer ")) {
jwt = authorizationHeader.substring(7);
username = jwtUtil.extractUsername(jwt);
        }

        if (username != null &&
 SecurityContextHolder.getContext().
getAuthentication() == null) {
UserDetails userDetails =
this.userDetailsService.
loadUserByUsername(username);
if (jwtUtil.validateToken(jwt,
userDetails)) {
UsernamePassword
AuthenticationToken
authenticationToken =
new UsernamePassword
AuthenticationToken
(userDetails, null, userDetails.
getAuthorities());
SecurityContextHolder.getContext().
setAuthentication
(authenticationToken);
            }
        }

        chain.doFilter(request, response);
    }
}
```

Add this filter to the **Spring Security** configuration to ensure all incoming requests are processed through the JWT validation filter.

4. Role-Based Access Control (RBAC)

Authorization is the process of controlling what actions an authenticated user is allowed to perform. **Role-Based Access Control (RBAC)** is a common approach where users are assigned roles, and each role has a set of permissions.

Step 1: Define User Roles

Add roles to the User model to define the level of access a user has:

```java
Copy code
public enum Role {
    USER,
    ADMIN
}

@Entity
public class User {
    // Other fields...

    @Enumerated(EnumType.STRING)
    private Role role;

    // Getters and setters...
}
```

Step 2: Use Annotations to Protect Endpoints

Spring Security allows you to use annotations to control access to specific methods based on the user's role. For example:

```java
Copy code
@RestController
@RequestMapping("/api/admin")
public class AdminController {

    @PreAuthorize("hasRole('ADMIN')")
    @GetMapping("/users")
    public List<User> getAllUsers() {
        // Only accessible by users
with the ADMIN role
        return userService.getAllUsers();
    }
```

```
}
```

The @PreAuthorize("hasRole('ADMIN')") annotation ensures that only users with the **ADMIN** role can access the /users endpoint.

Step 3: Configure Method Security

To use method-level security annotations like @PreAuthorize, add the following configuration to your Spring Boot application:

```java
Copy code
@EnableGlobalMethodSecurity(prePostEnabled = true)
public class SecurityConfig extends WebSecurityConfigurerAdapter {
    // Other security configurations...
}
```

Securely Consuming APIs in React

On the client side, security involves securely managing authentication tokens, protecting sensitive data, and making secure requests to the server. This section covers how to securely manage JWT tokens in a React application and how to send authenticated requests to the Spring Boot API.

1. Storing JWT Tokens

Once the JWT token is received from the backend after a successful login, it needs to be stored securely. There are two common places to store JWT tokens:

- **Local Storage**: Stores data on the client side, but is vulnerable to XSS attacks.
- **HTTP-Only Cookies**: These cookies are set by the server and are more secure as they cannot be accessed by JavaScript.

For better security, you should use **HTTP-only cookies** to store JWT tokens and rely on the server to handle setting and reading these cookies.

2. Sending Authenticated Requests

When consuming secured RESTful APIs, you need to include the JWT token in the **Authorization** header of every request.

Using Axios to Send Authenticated Requests

Install **Axios** if you haven't already:

```bash
Copy code
npm install axios
```

Configure Axios to include the JWT token in the Authorization header:

```javascript
Copy code
import axios from 'axios';

const token = localStorage.
getItem('token'); // Replace with cookie-based token retrieval if
using cookies

const axiosInstance = axios.create({
    baseURL: 'http://localhost:8080/api',
    headers: {
        'Authorization': `Bearer ${token}`
    }
});

export default axiosInstance;
```

Now, you can use axiosInstance to make authenticated requests to the API:

```javascript
Copy code
axiosInstance.get('/users')
    .then(response => {
        console.log('Users:', response.data);
    })
    .catch(error => {
```

```
        console.error
('Error fetching users:', error);
    });
```

3. Handling Expired Tokens

JWT tokens have an expiration date, and you need to handle token expiry gracefully on the client side. When a token expires, the API will return a **401 Unauthorized** response. In such cases, you can either prompt the user to log in again or refresh the token if your backend supports it.

Intercepting Responses to Handle Expired Tokens

You can use Axios interceptors to automatically handle **401 Unauthorized** responses:

```javascript
Copy code
axiosInstance.interceptors.response.use(
    response => response,
    error => {
        if (error.response && error.
response.status === 401) {
            // Redirect to login or refresh token
            window.location.href = '/login';
        }
        return Promise.reject(error);
    }
);
```

Implementing HTTPS and Secure Communication

HTTPS is crucial for securing the data exchanged between the client and server. It encrypts data transmitted over the network, preventing attackers from intercepting and reading sensitive information.

1. Generating an SSL Certificate

To enable HTTPS in Spring Boot, you need an **SSL certificate**. For development purposes, you can create a self-signed certificate using tools like **Java Keytool**.

```bash
bash
Copy code
keytool -genkeypair -alias mycert
-keyalg RSA -keystore keystore.
jks -keysize 2048
```

The above command generates a **keystore** containing an SSL certificate.

Chapter 12: Advanced Authorization Techniques and Role-Based Access Control (RBAC) in Spring Boot and React

In modern applications, controlling access to resources is just as important as authenticating users. Authorization ensures that users have permission to perform specific actions based on their roles or attributes. In a full-stack development scenario with Spring Boot and React, implementing a comprehensive authorization strategy that handles both backend resource protection and frontend route guarding is essential.

I n this chapter, we will explore advanced authorization techniques, focusing on **Role-Based Access Control (RBAC), Permission-Based Authorization**, and using **JWT (JSON Web Tokens)** to enforce security policies in a full-stack application. By the end of this chapter, you will understand how to create secure routes in React, enforce granular authorization on backend services, and integrate these features to build a robust, secure system.

Understanding Authorization and Role-Based Access Control

Authorization is the process of determining what actions a user can perform after they have been authenticated. This usually involves checking the user's role or permissions and deciding if they have the right to access a particular resource or perform a specific action.

Role-Based Access Control (RBAC) is a popular authorization model that assigns permissions to roles rather than directly to users. A user can have one or more roles, and each role has a set of permissions.

Benefits of RBAC:

1. **Simplified Administration**: Roles are easier to manage than individual user permissions, especially in systems with many users.
2. **Scalability**: Adding new users or permissions is straightforward—just assign the user to an appropriate role.
3. **Security**: Ensures that users only have access to the resources they need to perform their duties.

Key Concepts in RBAC:

- **Roles**: Represent groups of permissions, e.g., ADMIN, USER, EDITOR.
- **Permissions**: Define what actions a role can perform, e.g., CRE-ATE_USER, VIEW_REPORTS.
- **Users**: Individuals who are assigned roles.

Implementing RBAC in Spring Boot

In a backend managed by Spring Boot, RBAC can be implemented using **Spring Security** by assigning different authorities or roles to users and securing endpoints accordingly.

Step 1: Defining User Roles and Permissions

First, update your User entity to include roles. This can be done using a Role enum or a separate entity if you want more flexibility.

User Entity Example:

```java
Copy code
@Entity
public class User {

    @Id
    @GeneratedValue(strategy = GenerationType.IDENTITY)
    private Long id;

    private String username;
    private String password;

    @ElementCollection(fetch = FetchType.EAGER)
    @Enumerated(EnumType.STRING)
    private Set<Role> roles = new HashSet<>();

    // Getters and setters
}
```

Role Enum Example:

```java
Copy code
public enum Role {
    USER,
    ADMIN,
    EDITOR
}
```

In this example, each user has a set of roles. These roles determine what the user can do within the system.

Step 2: Configuring Security for Roles

In the Spring Security configuration, configure access based on roles by using the hasRole() method to restrict access to certain endpoints.

Security Configuration Example:

```java
Copy code
@Configuration
@EnableWebSecurity
public class SecurityConfig extends WebSecurityConfigurerAdapter {

    @Override
    protected void configure(HttpSecurity http) throws Exception {
        http.csrf().disable()
            .authorizeRequests()
            .antMatchers("/api/admin/**").hasRole("ADMIN")
            .antMatchers("/api/editor/**").hasAnyRole("EDITOR",
            "ADMIN")
            .antMatchers("/api/user/**").hasRole("USER")
            .anyRequest().authenticated()
            .and()
            .sessionManagement().
sessionCreationPolicy
(SessionCreationPolicy.STATELESS);
    }
}
```

In this example:

- Endpoints starting with /api/admin/ are restricted to users with the ADMIN role.
- Endpoints starting with /api/editor/ can be accessed by users with either the EDITOR or ADMIN role.
- Endpoints starting with /api/user/ are accessible only to users with the USER role.

Step 3: Storing Roles in JWT Tokens

When a user logs in, a **JWT** token is generated. This token can store the user's roles, which will be used for authorization on subsequent requests.

Updating the JWT Utility to Include Roles:

```java
Copy code
@Component
public class JwtUtil {

    private String SECRET_KEY = "mysecretkey";

    public String generateToken(UserDetails userDetails) {
        Map<String, Object> claims = new HashMap<>();
        claims.put("roles", userDetails.getAuthorities());
        return createToken(claims, userDetails.getUsername());
    }

    private String createToken(Map<String, Object> claims, String
    subject) {
        return Jwts.builder()
            .setClaims(claims)
            .setSubject(subject)
            .setIssuedAt(new Date(System.currentTimeMillis()))
            .setExpiration(new Date
(System.currentTimeMillis() +
1000 * 60 * 60 * 10)) // 10 hours expiration
            .signWith
(SignatureAlgorithm.HS256, SECRET_KEY)
            .compact();
```

```
    }
}
```

The roles are added to the claims in the JWT token. On the server side, these roles are extracted and used to determine whether a user has permission to access a specific endpoint.

Step 4: Extracting Roles from JWT Token in Request Filter

The JWT filter is updated to extract the roles from the token and set the authorities accordingly.

JWT Request Filter:

```java
Copy code
public class JwtRequestFilter extends OncePerRequestFilter {

    @Autowired
    private JwtUtil jwtUtil;

    @Autowired
    private UserDetailsServiceImpl userDetailsService;

    @Override
    protected void doFilterInternal
(HttpServletRequest request, HttpServletResponse response,
FilterChain chain)
        throws ServletException, IOException {

        final String authorizationHeader =
        request.getHeader("Authorization");

        String username = null;
        String jwt = null;

        if (authorizationHeader != null &&
        authorizationHeader.startsWith("Bearer ")) {
            jwt = authorizationHeader.substring(7);
            username = jwtUtil.extractUsername(jwt);
```

```
        }

        if (username != null &&
SecurityContextHolder.getContext().
getAuthentication() == null) {
            UserDetails userDetails = this.userDetailsService.
loadUserByUsername(username);
            if (jwtUtil.validateToken
(jwt, userDetails)) {
UsernamePasswordAuthenticationToken
authentication =
new UsernamePasswordAuthenticationToken(
                    userDetails, null,
                    userDetails.getAuthorities());
authentication.setDetails(new WebAuthenticationDetailsSource().
buildDetails(request));
SecurityContextHolder.getContext().
setAuthentication(authentication);
            }
        }

        chain.doFilter(request, response);
    }
}
```

The userDetails.getAuthorities() method retrieves the roles from the UserDetails object and attaches them to the authentication object, allowing role-based access control.

Securing React Frontend with Role-Based Authorization

On the frontend, securing routes and components based on user roles is just as important as securing the backend. **React Router** can be used to create protected routes that only authorized users can access.

1. Creating a Private Route Component

A **PrivateRoute** component can be used to guard specific routes so that only authenticated users with the correct role can access them.

PrivateRoute Component Example:

```javascript
javascript
Copy code
import React from 'react';
import { Route, Redirect } from 'react-router-dom';

const PrivateRoute = ({ component: Component, roles, ...rest }) =>
{
    const currentUser = JSON.parse(localStorage.getItem('user'));

    return (
        <Route
            {...rest}
            render={props => {
                if (!currentUser) {
                    // User is not logged in
return <Redirect to={{ pathname:
'/login', state:
{ from: props.location } }} />;
                }

// Check if user has the required role
if (roles && !roles.includes
(currentUser.role)) {
                    // Role not authorized
return <Redirect to={{ pathname: '/' }} />;
                }

            // User is authenticated and authorized
                return <Component {...props} />;
            }}
        />
    );
};

export default PrivateRoute;
```

In this example:

- The currentUser is retrieved from **localStorage**. This should contain the user's information, including roles, if they are logged in.

- The roles prop allows you to specify which roles can access the route. If the user's role doesn't match, they are redirected.

2. Protecting Routes with PrivateRoute

You can use the PrivateRoute component in your **React Router** configuration to protect routes.

Example Route Configuration:

```javascript
Copy code
import { BrowserRouter as Router, Route, Switch } from
'react-router-dom';
import Home from './components/Home';
import AdminDashboard from './components/AdminDashboard';
import UserDashboard from './components/UserDashboard';
import Login from './components/Login';
import PrivateRoute from './components/PrivateRoute';

const App = () => (
    <Router>
        <Switch>
            <Route path="/login" component={Login} />
            <PrivateRoute path=
"/admin" roles={['ADMIN']}
component={AdminDashboard} />
            <PrivateRoute path=
"/user" roles={['USER', 'ADMIN']}
 component={UserDashboard} />
            <Route path="/" component={Home} />
        </Switch>
    </Router>
);

export default App;
```

In this configuration:

- The /admin route is protected and only accessible by users with the

ADMIN role.

- The /user route can be accessed by users with either the USER or ADMIN role.
- If a user without the required role tries to access a protected route, they will be redirected.

3. Handling JWT Tokens on the Frontend

The JWT token received from the backend after a successful login must be stored securely on the client-side. This token is sent in the Authorization header for subsequent requests to protected endpoints.

Example of Storing and Sending JWT Token:

```javascript
Copy code
import axios from 'axios';

const loginUser = async (username, password) => {
    try {
        const response = await axios.post('/api/authenticate',
{ username, password });
        const token = response.data.token;

        // Store user details and token in local storage
        localStorage.setItem
('user', JSON.stringify({
            username,
            token,
            role: response.data.role
        }));

        // Set Authorization header for future requests
        axios.defaults.headers.
common['Authorization'] = `Bearer ${token}`;
    } catch (error) {
        console.error('Login failed:', error);
    }
};
```

In this example:

- The token and user information are stored in **localStorage** for later use.
- The **Authorization** header is set globally for all Axios requests, ensuring that every request to a protected endpoint includes the token.

Fine-Grained Authorization with Permission-Based Access Control

In addition to RBAC, you can implement **Permission-Based Access Control** for more granular control over what users can do within your application. Unlike RBAC, where permissions are linked to roles, **permissions** are assigned individually to users or roles.

1. Updating User Entity to Include Permissions

Instead of just roles, you can add a **permissions** field to the User entity.

User Entity with Permissions:

```java
Copy code
@Entity
public class User {

    @Id
    @GeneratedValue(strategy = GenerationType.IDENTITY)
    private Long id;

    private String username;
    private String password;

    @ElementCollection(fetch = FetchType.EAGER)
    @Enumerated(EnumType.STRING)
    private Set<Role> roles = new HashSet<>();

    @ElementCollection(fetch = FetchType.EAGER)
    private Set<String> permissions = new HashSet<>();

    // Getters and setters
}
```

2. Implementing Permission-Based Security

You can use permissions in conjunction with roles to determine what actions a user can perform. For example, you can use custom methods to check if a user has the required permission before executing an operation.

Permission Check Example:

```java
Copy code
@Service
public class ProductService {

    @Autowired
    private UserRepository userRepository;

    @Autowired
    private JwtUtil jwtUtil;

    public Product createProduct(String token, Product product) {
        String username = jwtUtil.
extractUsername(token);
        User user = userRepository.
findByUsername(username)
                .orElseThrow(() -> new
                ResourceNotFoundException("User not found"));

        if (!user.getPermissions().
contains("CREATE_PRODUCT")) {
            throw new AccessDeniedException
("You do not have permission to create products");
        }

        // Create the product
        return productRepository.save(product);
    }
}
```

In this example, the **createProduct** method checks if the user has the CREATE_PRODUCT permission before allowing them to create a product.

3. Securing React Components Based on Permissions

On the frontend, you can also enforce permissions by conditionally rendering components based on the user's permissions.

Example of Component Permission Check:

```javascript
Copy code
const CreateProductButton = () => {
    const currentUser = JSON.parse(localStorage.getItem('user'));

    if (currentUser &&
currentUser.permissions.
includes('CREATE_PRODUCT')) {
        return <button>Create Product</button>;
    }

    return null; // User does not have
permission to see this button
};
```

In this example, the **CreateProductButton** is only rendered if the user has the CREATE_PRODUCT permission.

Conclusion

This chapter explored advanced authorization techniques, focusing on **Role-Based Access Control (RBAC), Permission-Based Access Control**, and the integration of JWT tokens for authentication in a **Spring Boot** and **React** full-stack application. We implemented role-based security at both the backend and frontend levels to ensure that users only access the resources and routes they are authorized to use.

By leveraging Spring Security and JWTs on the backend,

Chapter 13: Advanced Full Stack Features—Real-Time Communication and Deployment Strategies

I n modern web applications, real-time capabilities and an efficient deployment strategy are key components that significantly impact the user experience and operational efficiency. This chapter focuses on adding **real-time features** to full-stack applications using technologies like **WebSockets, Server-Sent Events (SSE)**, and **STOMP**. We will also dive into **DevOps best practices**, covering continuous integration/continuous deployment (**CI/CD**) strategies, containerization with **Docker**, and deploying applications in the cloud using **Kubernetes**.

By the end of this chapter, you'll understand how to create applications that provide seamless real-time updates to users and how to deploy those applications to production environments using the latest industry best practices.

Real-Time Communication in Full Stack Applications

Real-time communication has become a core feature in modern web applications. Features like live notifications, chat applications, collaborative tools, and dashboards often require real-time updates, meaning that the client needs to be informed of server-side changes immediately. Achieving this kind of interaction can be done through several technologies like **WebSockets,**

Server-Sent Events (SSE), and STOMP over WebSockets.

1. Understanding Real-Time Communication Technologies

WebSockets

WebSockets provide a full-duplex communication channel over a single, long-lived connection. This is in contrast to HTTP, which is stateless and typically requires a new connection for each request/response cycle. With WebSockets, both the client and server can send data at any time.

Server-Sent Events (SSE)

Server-Sent Events are a one-way communication protocol where the server can send real-time updates to the client, but the client cannot send data back to the server through the same connection. SSE is useful for use cases like live dashboards, live news feeds, or notifications.

STOMP over WebSockets

STOMP (Simple Text Oriented Messaging Protocol) is a messaging protocol that can be used over WebSockets to provide structured real-time communication. This is particularly useful for chat applications, where clients need to subscribe to specific topics to receive messages.

Implementing WebSockets in Spring Boot

Spring Boot has excellent support for WebSockets and provides easy-to-use annotations to build a real-time communication layer. We will create a simple chat application as an example of WebSocket implementation in a Spring Boot application.

1. Setting Up Dependencies

To use WebSockets with Spring Boot, add the following dependency to your pom.xml:

```xml
Copy code
<dependency>
    <groupId>org.springframework.boot</groupId>
    <artifactId>spring-boot-starter-websocket</artifactId>
</dependency>
```

2. WebSocket Configuration

You need to configure WebSocket support in your Spring Boot application by creating a configuration class.

```java
Copy code
@Configuration
@EnableWebSocketMessageBroker
public class WebSocketConfig implements
WebSocketMessageBrokerConfigurer {

    @Override
    public void configureMessageBroker(MessageBrokerRegistry
    config) {
        config.enableSimpleBroker("/topic");
        config.setApplicationDestinationPrefixes("/app");
    }

    @Override
    public void registerStompEndpoints(StompEndpointRegistry
    registry) {
        registry.addEndpoint("/chat").withSockJS();
    }
}
```

In this example:

- **@EnableWebSocketMessageBroker**: Enables WebSocket message handling.
- **configureMessageBroker()**: Configures a simple message broker for the application. The /topic prefix is used to define broker topics.
- **registerStompEndpoints()**: Registers a STOMP endpoint at /chat, enabling clients to connect.

3. Creating a Chat Controller

The controller is responsible for handling messages sent to specific destinations and broadcasting messages to subscribed clients.

```java
Copy code
@Controller
public class ChatController {

    @MessageMapping("/sendMessage")
    @SendTo("/topic/messages")
    public ChatMessage sendMessage(ChatMessage message) {
        return message;
    }
}
```

- **@MessageMapping("/sendMessage")**: This annotation maps messages sent to /app/sendMessage to the sendMessage() method.
- **@SendTo("/topic/messages")**: Indicates that the return value of the method should be broadcast to all clients subscribed to /topic/messages.

4. ChatMessage Model

The ChatMessage class represents the message being exchanged between clients.

```java
Copy code
public class ChatMessage {
    private String sender;
    private String content;

    // Getters and setters
}
```

5. Creating the Frontend Component for React

In the React frontend, you can use the **SockJS** and **StompJS** libraries to connect to the WebSocket endpoint.

Install Dependencies

```bash
Copy code
npm install sockjs-client stompjs
```

React WebSocket Example

```javascript
Copy code
import React, { useEffect, useState } from 'react';
import SockJS from 'sockjs-client';
import Stomp from 'stompjs';

const ChatApp = () => {
    const [messages, setMessages] = useState([]);
    const [messageContent, setMessageContent] = useState('');
    let stompClient = null;

    useEffect(() => {
        const socket = new SockJS('http://localhost:8080/chat');
        stompClient = Stomp.over(socket);

        stompClient.connect({}, () => {
            stompClient.subscribe('/topic/messages', (msg) => {
                if (msg.body) {
                    setMessages((prevMessages) =>
                    [...prevMessages, JSON.parse(msg.body)]);
                }
            });
        });

        return () => {
            if (stompClient) {
                stompClient.disconnect();
            }
        };
    }, []);

    const sendMessage = () => {
        const message = {
```

```
            sender: 'User1',
            content: messageContent,
        };
        stompClient.send('/app/sendMessage', {},
        JSON.stringify(message));
        setMessageContent('');
    };

    return (
        <div>
            <div className="chat-messages">
                {messages.map((msg, index) => (
                    <div key={index}>
                        <strong>{msg.sender}</strong>:
                        {msg.content}
                    </div>
                ))}
            </div>
            <input
                type="text"
                value={messageContent}
                onChange={(e) => setMessageContent(e.target.value)}
            />
            <button onClick={sendMessage}>Send</button>
        </div>
    );
};

export default ChatApp;
```

This code allows the client to connect to the server via WebSockets, send messages, and subscribe to updates.

DevOps Strategies for Full Stack Applications

Deploying full-stack applications to production involves setting up continuous integration and deployment pipelines, containerizing the application, and managing infrastructure in a way that ensures stability and scalability. **DevOps** practices are crucial for maintaining an efficient development and deployment lifecycle.

151

1. Continuous Integration and Continuous Deployment (CI/CD)

CI/CD is a DevOps practice that helps developers integrate their code into a shared repository frequently, followed by automated builds and tests. This ensures that code changes are tested and deployed seamlessly.

1.1 Setting Up CI/CD with Jenkins

Jenkins is an open-source automation tool used to set up CI/CD pipelines. It integrates with code repositories like **GitHub** to automatically build, test, and deploy applications.

Step 1: Install Jenkins

You can run Jenkins on a local machine or a server by downloading it from jenkins.io. Alternatively, you can use Docker to run Jenkins:

```bash
Copy code
docker run -p 8080:8080 -p 50000:50000 jenkins/jenkins:lts
```

Step 2: Configure Jenkins Pipeline

Create a **Jenkinsfile** in your project's root directory. The Jenkinsfile defines the pipeline steps.

```groovy
Copy code
pipeline {
    agent any
    stages {
        stage('Build') {
            steps {
                sh 'mvn clean package'
            }
        }
        stage('Test') {
            steps {
                sh 'mvn test'
            }
        }
```

```
    stage('Deploy') {
        steps {
            sh './deploy.sh'
        }
    }
}
}
```

- **Build**: Uses Maven to package the application.
- **Test**: Runs unit tests.
- **Deploy**: Executes a custom script (deploy.sh) to deploy the application.

Step 3: Connect Jenkins to GitHub

Add a webhook in your **GitHub** repository to trigger Jenkins jobs whenever changes are pushed. This will automate the CI/CD pipeline, building and testing your code for each new commit.

2. Containerizing Full Stack Applications with Docker

Docker is a popular containerization platform that allows developers to bundle their applications and dependencies into a portable container. Docker makes it easier to manage deployment environments and ensures consistency across different systems.

2.1 Creating a Dockerfile for Spring Boot

Create a **Dockerfile** to containerize the Spring Boot application.

```dockerfile
dockerfile
Copy code
# Start with an OpenJDK base image
FROM openjdk:11-jre-slim

# Add the JAR file to the container
COPY target/myapp.jar myapp.jar

# Run the JAR file
ENTRYPOINT ["java", "-jar", "/myapp.jar"]
```

Build the Docker image using the following command:

```bash
Copy code
docker build -t myapp:latest .
```

2.2 Creating a Dockerfile for React

For the React application, create a Dockerfile to build and serve the frontend.

```dockerfile
Copy code
# Use Node.js to build the React app
FROM node:14 AS build

WORKDIR /app

COPY package*.json ./
RUN npm install

COPY . .
RUN npm run build

# Use Nginx to serve the static files
FROM nginx:alpine

COPY --from=build /app/build /usr/share/nginx/html
```

This Dockerfile first builds the React app and then uses **Nginx** to serve the static files.

2.3 Running the Docker Containers

To run the Spring Boot and React applications together, you can use **Docker Compose**. Create a **docker-compose.yml** file:

```yaml
yaml
Copy code
version: '3'
services:
  backend:
    image: myapp:latest
    build:
      context: .
      dockerfile: Dockerfile-backend
    ports:
      - "8080:8080"
  frontend:
    image: myreactapp:latest
    build:
      context: .
      dockerfile: Dockerfile-frontend
    ports:
      - "3000:80"
```

Use the following command to start the containers:

```bash
bash
Copy code
docker-compose up
```

This setup will run both the backend and frontend services in separate Docker containers, making it easier to manage and deploy.

3. Deploying to Kubernetes for Production

Kubernetes is an open-source container orchestration platform that helps automate the deployment, scaling, and management of containerized applications. Using Kubernetes, you can deploy your full stack application in a highly available and scalable environment.

3.1 Setting Up a Kubernetes Cluster

Google Kubernetes Engine (GKE), **Amazon Elastic Kubernetes Service (EKS)**, and **Azure Kubernetes Service (AKS)** are managed Kubernetes services that provide an easy way to create and manage Kubernetes clusters.

You can also use **Minikube** to set up a local Kubernetes cluster for development and testing purposes.

Install Minikube by following the official documentation here.

Start the cluster:

```bash
Copy code
minikube start
```

3.2 Creating Kubernetes Deployment and Service Manifests

Create a deployment manifest to define how your application should be deployed on Kubernetes.

deployment.yml

```yaml
Copy code
apiVersion: apps/v1
kind: Deployment
metadata:
  name: spring-boot-deployment
spec:
  replicas: 3
  selector:
    matchLabels:
      app: spring-boot-app
  template:
    metadata:
      labels:
        app: spring-boot-app
    spec:
      containers:
        - name: spring-boot-container
          image: myapp:latest
          ports:
            - containerPort: 8080
```

In this example:

- **replicas**: Defines how many instances (pods) of the application to run.
- **image**: Specifies the Docker image to use.

Create a **Service** manifest to expose the application.
service.yml

```yaml
Copy code
apiVersion: v1
kind: Service
metadata:
  name: spring-boot-service
spec:
  selector:
    app: spring-boot-app
  ports:
    - protocol: TCP
      port: 80
      targetPort: 8080
  type: LoadBalancer
```

Deploy the application to Kubernetes using the following command:

```bash
Copy code
kubectl apply -f deployment.yml
kubectl apply -f service.yml
```

This command creates both the deployment and the service, which exposes the application to the internet.

3.3 Horizontal Pod Autoscaling

Kubernetes Horizontal Pod Autoscaler (HPA) can automatically scale the number of pods in your deployment based on resource usage (e.g., CPU utilization).

Create an **HPA** for the Spring Boot deployment:

```yaml
yaml
Copy code
apiVersion: autoscaling/v1
kind: HorizontalPodAutoscaler
metadata:
  name: spring-boot-hpa
spec:
  scaleTargetRef:
    apiVersion: apps/v1
    kind: Deployment
    name: spring-boot-deployment
  minReplicas: 2
  maxReplicas: 10
  targetCPUUtilizationPercentage: 70
```

The HPA will maintain between 2 and 10 replicas of the application, scaling up or down based on CPU utilization.

Conclusion

In this chapter, we covered advanced features for building full stack applications with **Spring Boot** and **React**. We explored adding **real-time communication** capabilities using **WebSockets** and **STOMP**, allowing us to build interactive features like chat applications and live notifications.

We then moved on to **DevOps best practices**, starting with setting up **CI/CD pipelines** using **Jenkins**. We also covered **containerizing** full stack applications using **Docker** and deploying them with **Kubernetes**, leveraging the power of container orchestration for automated scaling, reliability, and ease of management.

With these tools and strategies, you can build sophisticated, interactive applications that not only provide an excellent user experience but are also easily deployable and scalable in production environments. In the next chapter, we will focus on monitoring, logging, and troubleshooting full stack applications, ensuring that they run smoothly and are easy to maintain.

Chapter 14: Monitoring, Logging, and Troubleshooting Full Stack Applications

To maintain a high-quality, scalable, and reliable full stack application, effective monitoring, logging, and troubleshooting practices are essential. These components allow you to proactively detect issues, maintain system health, and ensure a smooth user experience even as your application scales. This chapter focuses on how to implement comprehensive monitoring, logging, and troubleshooting mechanisms for Spring Boot and React applications using tools like Prometheus, Grafana, Elastic Stack (ELK), Datadog, and best practices for identifying and resolving production issues.

Why Monitoring and Logging Are Critical for Full Stack Applications
The combination of monitoring and logging provides a detailed understanding of your application's state, performance, and behavior, both at the backend (Spring Boot) and frontend (React).

Monitoring vs. Logging

- **Monitoring**: This involves tracking and collecting performance metrics such as CPU usage, memory consumption, and request response times to identify any abnormal behavior or bottlenecks in the application.
- **Logging**: This is the practice of recording events and activities within the application, such as user actions, system activities, errors, and debugging information. Logs are essential for troubleshooting and for creating an audit trail.

Key Benefits:

- **Proactive Detection**: Monitoring helps detect anomalies or bottlenecks before they lead to system failure.
- **Detailed Diagnostics**: Logging helps identify the root cause of issues after they occur.
- **Performance Optimization**: Analyzing monitoring metrics allows

you to identify areas that need optimization, leading to better resource management and user experience.

- **Auditing and Compliance**: Logs provide an audit trail that can be used for security compliance and forensic analysis.

Monitoring Full Stack Applications with Prometheus and Grafana

Prometheus and **Grafana** are widely used open-source tools for monitoring and visualization. **Prometheus** is a powerful time-series database that collects metrics from your application, while **Grafana** allows you to create beautiful, interactive dashboards for visualizing those metrics.

1. Setting Up Prometheus for Backend Monitoring

Prometheus can be used to monitor the Spring Boot backend. **Spring Boot Actuator** provides an endpoint that exposes application metrics in a format that Prometheus can scrape.

Step 1: Enable Spring Boot Actuator Metrics

Add the **Spring Boot Actuator** dependency to your pom.xml:

```xml
Copy code
<dependency>
    <groupId>org.springframework.boot</groupId>
    <artifactId>spring-boot-starter-actuator</artifactId>
</dependency>
```

Configure Actuator to expose metrics at /actuator/prometheus by adding the following to application.yml:

```yaml
Copy code
management:
  endpoints:
    web:
      exposure:
        include: health, metrics, prometheus
```

Step 2: Install and Configure Prometheus

Download and install **Prometheus** from prometheus.io. Create a **prometheus.yml** configuration file:

```yaml
yaml
Copy code
global:
  scrape_interval: 15s

scrape_configs:
  - job_name: 'spring-boot'
    static_configs:
      - targets: ['localhost:8080']  # Replace with the actual
        address and port of your Spring Boot application
```

Start Prometheus with the configuration:

```bash
bash
Copy code
./prometheus --config.file=prometheus.yml
```

Prometheus will now scrape metrics from your Spring Boot application every 15 seconds.

2. Visualizing Metrics with Grafana

Grafana is used to visualize the metrics collected by Prometheus.

Step 1: Install Grafana

Download and install **Grafana** from grafana.com. Once installed, start Grafana and navigate to http://localhost:3000 in your browser.

Step 2: Connect Prometheus as a Data Source

To connect **Prometheus** to **Grafana**:

1. Go to **Configuration > Data Sources**.
2. Click **Add data source**.
3. Select **Prometheus** and provide the URL of your Prometheus server (http://localhost:9090).

Step 3: Create Dashboards

You can create custom dashboards or import pre-built dashboards from the **Grafana Dashboard Library**. A typical dashboard might include:

- **HTTP request latency.**
- **CPU and memory usage.**
- **Database connection pool statistics.**
- **Error rate per endpoint.**

3. Frontend Monitoring with Google Analytics and Lighthouse

The **React** frontend also needs monitoring to track user behavior, page performance, and overall user experience.

Step 1: Google Analytics

Google Analytics allows you to track user interactions, page views, and the flow of user activity throughout your application. You can integrate Google Analytics into a React application using the **React-GA** library:

```bash
bash
Copy code
npm install react-ga
```

Configure Google Analytics in your application:

```javascript
javascript
Copy code
import ReactGA from 'react-ga';

ReactGA.initialize('YOUR_GOOGLE_ANALYTICS_TRACKING_ID');
ReactGA.pageview(window.location.pathname +
window.location.search);
```

Step 2: Lighthouse for Performance Metrics

Lighthouse is an open-source tool for auditing web performance, SEO, accessibility, and more. You can use Lighthouse in the Chrome DevTools to get a report on:

- **Page load speed.**
- **JavaScript execution time.**
- **Opportunities to optimize images.**

These metrics provide insight into areas where the React frontend can be optimized for a better user experience.

Centralized Logging with the ELK Stack

For comprehensive logging, you can use the **ELK Stack** (Elasticsearch, Logstash, and Kibana) to centralize, search, and visualize logs from both the Spring Boot backend and the React frontend.

1. Overview of the ELK Stack

- **Elasticsearch**: A distributed search and analytics engine used to store logs.
- **Logstash**: A data processing pipeline that collects logs, processes them, and forwards them to Elasticsearch.
- **Kibana**: A visualization tool used to explore and analyze the logs stored in Elasticsearch.

2. Installing and Configuring the ELK Stack

Step 1: Installing Elasticsearch

Download and install **Elasticsearch** from elastic.co. Start Elasticsearch using:

```bash
Copy code
./bin/elasticsearch
```

Step 2: Installing Logstash

Download and install **Logstash**. Create a configuration file (logstash.conf) to specify where to collect logs and how to process them:

```bash
Copy code
input {
  file {
    path => "/var/log/spring-boot/*.log"
    start_position => "beginning"
  }
}

output {
  elasticsearch {
    hosts => ["localhost:9200"]
  }
}
```

Start Logstash with the configuration:

```bash
Copy code
./bin/logstash -f logstash.conf
```

Step 3: Installing Kibana

Download and install **Kibana**. Start Kibana using:

```bash
Copy code
./bin/kibana
```

Access Kibana at http://localhost:5601 and set up an index pattern to explore the logs collected in Elasticsearch.

3. Logging Best Practices for Spring Boot

3.1 Configuring Log Levels

Set the appropriate log level (e.g., INFO, DEBUG, WARN, ERROR) in the application.yml file:

```yaml
yaml
Copy code
logging:
  level:
    root: INFO
    com.example: DEBUG
```

- **DEBUG**: Use for development to log detailed information about the flow.
- **INFO**: Use for high-level information that helps track application behavior.
- **WARN/ERROR**: Use for logging potential issues or critical failures.

3.2 Structuring Logs for Better Searchability

Logs should be structured for easy parsing by tools like Logstash. **JSON** is a common format for structured logs.

```java
java
Copy code
private static final Logger logger =
LoggerFactory.getLogger(MyService.class);

public void myMethod() {
    Map<String, Object> logData = new HashMap<>();
    logData.put("event", "user_login");
    logData.put("userId", 12345);
    logData.put("status", "success");

    logger.info("{}", new JSONObject(logData).toString());
}
```

Structured logs are easy to search and analyze, especially when using Elasticsearch.

3.3 Capturing Contextual Information

Ensure logs contain enough contextual information, such as:

166

- **Request ID**: A unique identifier for each request, useful for tracing.
- **User ID**: If applicable, include the user ID to understand user-specific issues.
- **Timestamp**: Logs should always contain timestamps to understand when an event occurred.

Setting Up Alerting and Proactive Monitoring

Proactive monitoring involves setting up alerts to be notified of any issues before they affect users. Tools like **Prometheus Alertmanager**, **Grafana Alerts**, and **Datadog** can be used to achieve this.

1. Using Prometheus Alertmanager

Alertmanager is part of the Prometheus ecosystem and is used to handle alerts generated by Prometheus.

Step 1: Configure Alerting Rules in Prometheus

Create an alerting rule to monitor specific metrics. For example, to trigger an alert if the average response time exceeds a threshold:

```yaml
Copy code
groups:
  - name: spring-boot-alerts
    rules:
      - alert: HighResponseTime
        expr: http_server_requests_seconds_sum /
        http_server_requests_seconds_count > 0.5
        for: 1m
        labels:
          severity: warning
        annotations:
          summary: "High Response Time Detected"
          description: "The average response time has exceeded 0.5
          seconds for
```

Chapter 15: Advanced Deployment Strategies and Cloud Architecture for Full Stack Applications

I n the increasingly complex world of software development, understanding advanced deployment strategies and how to leverage cloud
architectures is critical for ensuring that applications are scalable,
resilient, and efficient. In this chapter, we will cover advanced deployment
strategies for **Spring Boot** and **React** applications, including **blue-
green deployments**, **canary releases**, **rolling updates**, and **immutable
infrastructure**. We will also explore best practices for cloud architecture,
focusing on popular platforms like **AWS**, **Google Cloud**, and **Azure**.

We will guide you through building resilient architectures using **microservices**, **serverless computing**, and **container orchestration** to achieve
better scalability and fault tolerance.

Deployment Strategies for Full Stack Applications

When deploying full stack applications to production, choosing the right
deployment strategy is crucial for minimizing downtime, managing risks,
and improving the overall quality of the software. We will explore several
advanced deployment techniques, each with its benefits and trade-offs.

1. Blue-Green Deployment

Blue-green deployment is a strategy in which two identical environments,

Blue and **Green**, are maintained. One environment (e.g., Blue) is live and serving production traffic, while the other environment (e.g., Green) is idle and contains the new version of the application.

How It Works:

- **Step 1**: Deploy the new version of the application to the idle environment (e.g., Green).
- **Step 2**: Run acceptance tests in the Green environment.
- **Step 3**: Once tests pass, switch the router (e.g., a load balancer) to point to the Green environment.
- **Step 4**: The Blue environment can be used for rollback if any issues are detected.

Advantages:

- **Zero Downtime**: The switch from Blue to Green is instant, allowing for zero-downtime deployments.
- **Safe Rollback**: If there is an issue with the new deployment, traffic can be easily redirected to the previous environment.

Implementation Example on AWS:

On **AWS**, you can use **Elastic Load Balancers (ELB)** along with **EC2 instances**. The Blue environment may consist of a set of EC2 instances behind an ELB, while the Green environment has an identical configuration. You can use **Route 53** to switch traffic between Blue and Green environments.

2. Canary Releases

Canary releases allow you to gradually introduce a new version of your application to a subset of users, monitoring its impact before a full rollout. This strategy reduces the risk associated with deploying new features by limiting exposure initially.

How It Works:

- **Step 1**: Deploy the new version to a small percentage of users or instances.
- **Step 2**: Monitor metrics such as error rates, response times, and user

feedback.

- **Step 3**: Gradually increase the percentage of users using the new version until it is fully deployed.

Advantages:

- **Controlled Exposure**: You can minimize risk by releasing features to a small group before scaling up.
- **Real-User Feedback**: Canary releases allow for collecting real-user feedback and metrics.

Implementation Example on Kubernetes:

You can implement canary releases in **Kubernetes** using **service mesh** technologies like **Istio** or **Linkerd**, which allow you to control traffic splitting between different versions of the service. Istio's **VirtualService** lets you define rules for directing traffic, making it easy to control how much traffic is routed to each version.

```yaml
Copy code
apiVersion: networking.istio.io/v1alpha3
kind: VirtualService
metadata:
  name: myapp
spec:
  hosts:
    - myapp.example.com
  http:
    - route:
        - destination:
            host: myapp
            subset: v1
          weight: 80
        - destination:
            host: myapp
            subset: v2
```

```
weight: 20
```

In this example, 20% of traffic is directed to version v2, while the remaining 80% continues to use version v1.

3. Rolling Updates

Rolling updates involve gradually updating instances of an application while keeping the service running. This strategy is commonly used in container orchestration platforms like Kubernetes.

How It Works:

- **Step 1**: Update a subset of instances to the new version.
- **Step 2**: Once the subset is stable, update the next subset.
- **Step 3**: Repeat until all instances are running the new version.

Advantages:

- **No Downtime**: Rolling updates allow for gradual changes without taking the application offline.
- **Reduced Risk**: In case of an issue, updates can be paused to investigate before affecting all instances.

Implementation in Kubernetes:

In **Kubernetes**, a **Deployment** resource automatically manages rolling updates.

```yaml
Copy code
apiVersion: apps/v1
kind: Deployment
metadata:
  name: myapp
spec:
  replicas: 5
  strategy:
```

```
  type: RollingUpdate
  rollingUpdate:
    maxUnavailable: 1
    maxSurge: 1
template:
  metadata:
    labels:
      app: myapp
  spec:
    containers:
      - name: myapp
        image: myapp:latest
```

Here, Kubernetes will manage updating the application with one new pod at a time, ensuring that the application remains available during the update.

4. Immutable Infrastructure

Immutable infrastructure means that once a server or container is deployed, it is never modified. Instead, new versions are deployed to new infrastructure, and the old infrastructure is discarded.

How It Works:

- **Step 1**: Build a new infrastructure (e.g., virtual machine or container) with the updated application.
- **Step 2**: Deploy the new infrastructure and decommission the old one.
- **Step 3**: If a rollback is needed, simply redeploy the old version.

Advantages:

- **Consistency**: There are no configuration drift issues since infrastructure is rebuilt from scratch.
- **Simplified Rollback**: Rolling back simply means redeploying the old version of the infrastructure.

Implementation with Docker:

Docker makes immutable infrastructure easy. Instead of updating an existing container, you create a new Docker image and deploy it as a new container, discarding the old one.

```bash
Copy code
docker build -t myapp:v2 .
docker run -d --name myapp_v2 -p 8080:8080 myapp:v2
```

Using tools like **Terraform** and **AWS CloudFormation**, you can also create and manage immutable cloud infrastructure.

Cloud Architecture Best Practices for Full Stack Applications

Deploying full stack applications on the cloud brings numerous benefits, including scalability, reliability, and ease of management. Choosing the right cloud architecture can make or break your application's success.

1. Serverless Architecture

In a **serverless architecture**, you do not manage servers directly. Instead, you rely on managed services that automatically handle server provisioning, scaling, and maintenance. **AWS Lambda, Azure Functions**, and **Google Cloud Functions** are examples of serverless compute services.

Benefits:

- **Scalability**: Serverless services automatically scale based on demand.
- **Reduced Maintenance**: No need to manage servers, patch operating systems, or deal with scalability issues.
- **Cost Efficiency**: You pay only for what you use, with no idle costs.

Using AWS Lambda with Spring Boot:

You can use **AWS Lambda** to execute backend logic without provisioning servers. A typical use case is exposing AWS Lambda functions through **API Gateway**:

1. Create a Spring Boot service and use the **aws-serverless-java-container** library to deploy it as a Lambda function.
2. Use **API Gateway** to trigger the Lambda function on HTTP requests.

3. Deploy and test the service.

2. Microservices Architecture

A **microservices architecture** involves breaking down an application into smaller, independent services, each responsible for a specific business function. This architectural style is particularly beneficial for large applications, as it improves scalability and allows teams to work independently on different components.

Benefits:

- **Scalability**: Individual services can be scaled independently.
- **Fault Isolation**: Issues in one service are less likely to affect the entire application.
- **Technology Diversity**: Teams can choose the best technology for each service without impacting others.

Implementing Microservices with Kubernetes:

Kubernetes is ideal for managing microservices, as it provides features like service discovery, load balancing, and automated deployments.

Each microservice can be deployed as a separate **Deployment** in Kubernetes, and **Ingress Controllers** can route traffic to the appropriate microservice based on URLs.

3. Hybrid Cloud and Multi-Cloud Architecture

A **hybrid cloud** architecture involves using a combination of on-premises and cloud environments, while a **multi-cloud** architecture involves using services from multiple cloud providers like **AWS**, **Azure**, and **Google Cloud**.

Benefits:

- **Flexibility**: The ability to leverage the best services from different providers.
- **Vendor Lock-In Reduction**: Using multiple cloud providers reduces dependence on any single provider.
- **Risk Mitigation**: Distributing workloads across multiple clouds reduces

the impact of an outage at a single provider.

Implementing Multi-Cloud Strategies:

Terraform can be used to manage resources across multiple clouds using a single configuration file. For example, you can provision resources on both AWS and Azure from a single **Terraform script**:

```hcl
Copy code
provider "aws" {
  region = "us-west-1"
}

provider "azurerm" {
  features {}
}

resource "aws_instance" "web" {
  ami           = "ami-12345678"
  instance_type = "t2.micro"
}

resource "azurerm_virtual_machine" "web" {
  name                = "example-vm"
  resource_group_name = "example-resources"
  location            = "West US"
  network_interface_ids =
  ["${azurerm_network_interface.example.id}"]
  vm_size             = "Standard_DS1_v2"
}
```

This configuration allows you to manage resources in both AWS and Azure, providing a unified approach to multi-cloud deployments.

4. Edge Computing

Edge computing brings computation and data storage closer to the location where it is needed, reducing latency and improving performance for end-users. This is particularly important for applications requiring real-time processing, such as IoT or AR/VR applications.

Benefits:

- **Reduced Latency**: Data is processed closer to the source, resulting in faster response times.
- **Bandwidth Efficiency**: Less data is sent to centralized data centers, reducing bandwidth requirements.
- **Reliability**: Edge computing provides better fault tolerance, as processing happens closer to the user.

Using AWS Greengrass for Edge Computing:

AWS Greengrass allows you to run local compute, messaging, and data caching for connected devices. It extends AWS services to edge devices, enabling them to act on the data they generate locally while still using the cloud for management and storage.

Building Resilient Applications with Fault Tolerance and Redundancy

To build applications that are resilient to failures, it is crucial to implement fault-tolerance and redundancy strategies in your architecture.

1. Load Balancing and Auto Scaling

Load balancers distribute incoming traffic across multiple instances of your application to ensure no single instance is overwhelmed. **Auto Scaling** helps manage the number of instances based on demand, ensuring there are enough instances to handle traffic spikes.

Using AWS Auto Scaling and ELB:

1. Use an **Elastic Load Balancer (ELB)** to distribute traffic across multiple EC2 instances.
2. Configure **Auto Scaling Groups** to automatically adjust the number of instances based on CPU usage or incoming requests.
3. Define **Scaling Policies** to control how and when instances are added or removed.

2. Distributed Data Storage with Replication

Ensuring data availability involves using **distributed data storage** systems that provide replication and partitioning.

Database Replication:

- **Master-Slave Replication**: The **master** database handles all write operations, while **slave** databases replicate data from the master and handle read requests. This provides redundancy and improves read performance.
- **Multi-Master Replication**: All databases are **masters** and can handle both read and write operations. This is more complex to manage but provides better availability.

Chapter 16: Implementing High Availability and Disaster Recovery Strategies for Full Stack Applications

High availability and disaster recovery are two critical components for ensuring that modern applications can withstand failures, maintain service continuity, and quickly recover from unexpected disruptions. With businesses increasingly dependent on web applications for operations, it's essential that your **Spring Boot** and **React** full stack applications are built to handle failures gracefully and minimize downtime.

In this chapter, we'll cover advanced techniques to implement **high availability (HA)** and **disaster recovery (DR)** strategies. This includes designing a resilient architecture, employing multi-region and multi-availability zone deployments, utilizing cloud services for HA and DR, and defining appropriate **recovery point objectives (RPO)** and **recovery time objectives (RTO)**.

Understanding High Availability and Disaster Recovery

Before delving into specific techniques, it is important to understand what **high availability** and **disaster recovery** entail and how they contribute to application reliability.

High Availability (HA)

High availability refers to the practice of ensuring that an application or service remains available with minimal downtime. HA is achieved by reducing single points of failure and adding redundancy to the system so that it can continue to function in case of hardware or software failures.

Disaster Recovery (DR)

Disaster recovery focuses on restoring an application after a significant disruption, such as a natural disaster, major infrastructure failure, or a security breach. DR involves defining plans, strategies, and mechanisms to recover data and bring the system back online within an acceptable timeframe.

RPO and RTO

- **Recovery Point Objective (RPO)**: The maximum acceptable amount of data loss measured in time. For instance, if the RPO is 30 minutes, the system must be capable of recovering all data up to 30 minutes prior to a failure.
- **Recovery Time Objective (RTO)**: The target time within which systems and applications must be restored after a disaster to avoid significant business impact.

Designing Highly Available Architectures

High availability is about designing the infrastructure so that your services can continue operating even if individual components fail. There are several approaches to building a highly available system.

1. Multi-Availability Zone Deployment

In cloud environments, availability zones (AZs) are isolated locations within a region. Deploying your application across multiple AZs ensures that even if one AZ experiences a failure, your application can continue running.

How to Implement Multi-AZ Deployment:
Using AWS for Multi-AZ Deployment:

1. **Elastic Load Balancer (ELB)**: Use an **Elastic Load Balancer** to distribute traffic across instances in multiple AZs.
2. **Auto Scaling Groups**: Configure **Auto Scaling Groups** to launch instances across different AZs automatically. This ensures redundancy at all times.

3. **Database with Multi-AZ**: Amazon **RDS** allows you to set up a **Multi-AZ** database, where a secondary database instance is maintained in a separate AZ, ensuring redundancy and failover capabilities.

Using Kubernetes for Multi-AZ:

Kubernetes can also be used for deploying highly available applications. You can set up a Kubernetes cluster that spans multiple AZs. Nodes in different AZs ensure that application workloads are distributed across locations, maintaining resilience even if an entire AZ goes down.

2. Load Balancing

Load balancing is essential for distributing traffic across multiple instances or servers to ensure that no single server is overwhelmed.

Load Balancing Strategies:

- **Round Robin**: Distributes requests to servers in a circular manner.
- **Least Connections**: Routes the request to the server with the fewest active connections.
- **Geolocation-Based**: Routes requests based on the geographical proximity of the user to minimize latency.

Implementing Load Balancers in AWS:

Elastic Load Balancer (ELB) is commonly used to balance traffic between EC2 instances. AWS provides several types of load balancers, including **Application Load Balancer (ALB)** and **Network Load Balancer (NLB)**, each suited for different use cases.

```yaml
yaml
Copy code
apiVersion: networking.gke.io/v1
kind: Ingress
metadata:
  name: example-ingress
  annotations:
    kubernetes.io/ingress.class: "gce"
```

```
spec:
  rules:
    - host: "example.com"
      http:
        paths:
          - path: "/"
            backend:
              serviceName: example-service
              servicePort: 80
```

3. Redundancy at Multiple Levels

High availability requires redundancy at every level, from the application to the infrastructure. There are different types of redundancy:

Application-Level Redundancy:

In **microservices architectures**, redundancy can be achieved by running multiple instances of each microservice, often distributed across multiple AZs or regions.

Database Redundancy:

Database redundancy can be achieved by using **replication** strategies. In **MySQL**, for example, master-slave or master-master replication is used to ensure that data is copied to multiple nodes, thus preventing data loss and ensuring availability.

Network-Level Redundancy:

Network redundancy involves having multiple network paths and end-points to ensure there is no single point of failure. Cloud providers like **AWS** provide **Direct Connect** services to ensure highly available network connections.

Implementing Disaster Recovery Strategies

A good disaster recovery strategy aims to recover applications quickly and ensure minimal data loss after an unexpected disruption. Below, we discuss a few key DR approaches.

1. Backup and Restore

The simplest disaster recovery approach is to create periodic backups of critical data and restore them in case of a disaster. While this approach may have a longer recovery time, it is easy to implement and suitable for smaller applications.

AWS Backup Strategy:

1. **RDS Snapshots**: AWS **RDS** provides automated snapshots, which can be used to recover the database to a specific point in time.
2. **Amazon S3 Backup**: Use **Amazon S3** to store backup files of your application data.

```bash
Copy code
aws s3 cp /backup/myapp-backup.tar.gz s3://my-backups/
```

This command uploads a local backup to an S3 bucket.

2. Pilot Light

Pilot Light involves maintaining a minimal version of your environment in the cloud. In the event of a disaster, additional resources are launched from this minimal environment to take over all operations.

How to Implement Pilot Light on AWS:

- **Minimal Infrastructure**: Maintain a small, lightweight version of your infrastructure, such as a minimal **RDS** instance and critical EC2 instances.
- **Automated Scaling**: Use **Auto Scaling** to quickly spin up additional instances in case of a disaster.

3. Warm Standby

Warm Standby is an approach where a scaled-down version of your production environment is always running in another region or AZ. In case of a failure, this environment can be scaled up to take over full operations.

Using AWS for Warm Standby:

- **EC2 Instances**: Run a small number of **EC2** instances in a standby region with the same configuration as the production environment.
- **Load Balancer**: Set up an **Elastic Load Balancer** that can reroute traffic to the standby environment if needed.

4. Multi-Region Active-Active

Active-Active architecture involves running identical instances of your application in multiple regions, all serving live traffic. This architecture ensures maximum availability and reduces latency for users across different geographical locations.

Multi-Region Setup in AWS:

- **Route 53**: AWS **Route 53** provides **geolocation routing**, which directs users to the closest region, reducing latency.
- **DynamoDB Global Tables**: Use **DynamoDB Global Tables** for a multi-region, fully replicated NoSQL database, ensuring data consistency across regions.

5. Disaster Recovery Runbooks and Automation

A **disaster recovery runbook** is a documented procedure that outlines the steps necessary to recover from a disaster. Automating parts of the runbook can significantly reduce recovery times.

Using AWS Lambda for Automation:

AWS Lambda can be used to automate parts of the recovery process. For example, you can write a Lambda function that:

- Automatically spins up resources in a different region when a failure is detected.
- Triggers a **SNS** notification to inform the operations team of the failure.

6. Infrastructure as Code (IaC) for Disaster Recovery

Using **Infrastructure as Code (IaC)** tools like **Terraform** and **AWS Cloud-Formation** makes it easier to create, destroy, and replicate infrastructure in a disaster recovery scenario.

Example: Using Terraform for Disaster Recovery:

With Terraform, you can write a script that defines your infrastructure and deploys it in a different region with minimal effort:

```hcl
Copy code
provider "aws" {
  region = "us-west-1"
}

resource "aws_instance" "web" {
  ami           = "ami-12345678"
  instance_type = "t2.micro"
  availability_zone = "us-west-1a"
}
```

This script can be reused to create the infrastructure in different regions, helping in disaster recovery situations.

Database Disaster Recovery Best Practices

For highly available systems, it is crucial to ensure that your databases can quickly recover from failures and maintain data consistency.

1. Database Replication

Replication is the process of copying data from one database server (the master) to another (the slave). There are different types of database replication:

Master-Slave Replication:

The **master** server handles all write operations, while **slave** servers replicate data from the master and handle read operations. This not only provides redundancy but also improves read performance by offloading read traffic to slaves.

Multi-Master Replication:

Multi-master replication allows both master servers to handle read and write operations. This provides better availability, as any of the master servers can take over if one fails. However, managing consistency is more challenging compared to master-slave replication.

2. Database Snapshots

Database snapshots are point-in-time backups of your database, which can be restored to recover lost data.

RDS Snapshots on AWS:

AWS RDS allows you to take **manual snapshots** or set up **automated backups** to protect your data. In case of failure, you can restore from these snapshots and create a new RDS instance.

3. Cross-Region Replication for Disaster Recovery

For disaster recovery, it is important to replicate databases across regions.

Aurora Global Database:

Amazon Aurora provides **Global Database** functionality, which replicates data across multiple AWS regions. In case of a regional outage, the secondary region can be promoted to take over, providing fast recovery.

High Availability and DR for Stateless vs. Stateful Applications

Understanding the difference between **stateless** and **stateful** applications is crucial when planning high availability and disaster recovery strategies.

Stateless Applications

Stateless applications do not store any information about user sessions on the server. Each request is independent. Examples include:

- **REST APIs** that use tokens for authentication.
- **Microservices** where the state is managed externally (e.g., databases or caching layers).

HA and DR Considerations:

- **Auto Scaling**: Stateless applications can easily be scaled up or down without worrying about session persistence.
- **Load Balancing**: Traffic can be evenly distributed without worrying about which instance handles the request.

Stateful Applications

Stateful applications maintain information about client sessions. Examples include:

- **Databases** that store user information.
- **Chat applications** that store user conversations in memory.

HA and DR Considerations:

- **Session Persistence**: Load balancers need to be configured with **sticky sessions** to ensure that requests from the same client are routed to the same instance.
- **Replication**: Stateful components, like databases, require replication to ensure that data remains consistent across different instances or regions.

Using Redis for Session Management:

For applications that require statefulness, **Redis** can be used as a distributed in-memory store to maintain user sessions:

```yaml
yaml
Copy code
apiVersion: v1
kind: Pod
metadata:
  name: redis
  labels:
    app: redis
spec:
  containers:
    - name: redis
      image: redis:alpine
      ports:
        - containerPort: 6379
```

Redis helps manage sessions, making your application more resilient by ensuring session data is accessible across multiple instances.

Monitoring for High Availability and Disaster Recovery

Monitoring plays a critical role in high availability and disaster recovery by providing insights into system health, performance, and alerting teams of potential issues.

1. Health Checks for High Availability

Health checks are used to determine if instances of an application are functioning correctly. If an instance fails a health check, it is removed from the load balancer, ensuring that only healthy instances receive traffic.

AWS ELB Health Checks:

Elastic Load Balancer can be configured to run **health checks** on all registered instances:

```yaml
Copy code
healthCheck {
  healthyThreshold = 3
  unhealthyThreshold = 2
  timeout = 5
  interval = 30
}
```

2. Application-Level Health Checks

Spring Boot Actuator can be used to add health check endpoints that provide application-level health information:

```yaml
Copy code
management:
  endpoints:
    web:
      exposure:
        include: health, info
```

The /actuator/health endpoint provides information about the application's current health and can be used by monitoring tools to determine its availability.

3. Logging and Alerting for DR Readiness

Centralized logging with tools like **Elastic Stack (ELK)** or **Splunk** helps you identify issues faster by providing insights into system logs.

Alerting with Prometheus Alertmanager:

Configure **Prometheus Alertmanager** to send alerts when critical metrics (e.g., CPU usage, response times, error rates) reach a threshold:

```yaml
Copy code
groups:
  - name: availability-alerts
    rules:
      - alert: HighErrorRate
        expr: rate(http_requests_total{status=~"5.*"}[5m]) > 0.05
        for: 2m
        labels:
          severity: critical
        annotations:
          summary: "High 5xx Error Rate Detected"
```

Conclusion

In this chapter, we explored various strategies and practices to ensure **high availability (HA)** and **disaster recovery (DR)** for your full stack applications. We started by understanding the core concepts of HA and DR, including **Recovery Point Objective (RPO)** and **Recovery Time Objective (RTO)**. We then discussed how to design highly available architectures using **multi-availability zones**, **load balancing**, and **redundancy** at different levels of the application.

Next, we explored disaster recovery strategies such as **backup and restore, pilot light, warm standby**, and **multi-region active-active** architectures. We also examined database disaster recovery techniques, including **replication, snapshots**, and **cross-region replication**.

Finally, we covered how to ensure HA and DR for **stateless** versus **stateful** applications, the importance of monitoring, and how tools like **Prometheus, Elastic Load Balancer**, and **Spring Boot Actuator** can be used to implement effective health checks, monitoring, and alerting.

By implementing these strategies, you can build resilient applications that can withstand failures and quickly recover from unexpected disruptions, providing your users with a reliable and uninterrupted experience. In the next chapter, we will focus on building secure applications and explore best practices for protecting your full stack applications from security threats and vulnerabilities.

Conclusion: Bringing It All Together

B uilding a full stack application using **Spring Boot** and **React** is a challenging yet immensely rewarding journey that requires a deep understanding of both frontend and backend technologies. This book has taken you through every step of the development process, from setting up a reliable and performant backend, creating a seamless and dynamic frontend, to deploying your application in the cloud while ensuring high availability, scalability, and disaster resilience.

We began by diving into the core concepts of full stack development— understanding how **Spring Boot** and **React** complement each other, setting up development environments, and structuring code for optimal maintainability. By combining a strong Java backend with an interactive JavaScript frontend, you've learned to build a full-fledged, responsive web application that is both scalable and user-friendly.

A significant part of full stack development involves managing data. We explored the use of **Spring Data JPA** for efficient database interactions, including strategies for optimizing queries, using pagination, and leveraging projections to minimize data load. This ensured that your backend is capable of handling large volumes of data while maintaining fast response times. On the frontend side, **React** was used to consume these APIs, providing a seamless user experience by dynamically updating the UI in response to real-time changes.

Deploying a full stack application in a production environment requires more than just writing functional code. Throughout this book, we explored **deployment strategies** such as **rolling updates, blue-green deployments,** and **canary releases.** These techniques allow you to introduce new features while minimizing downtime and reducing risks. By leveraging containerization with **Docker** and orchestration with **Kubernetes,** you gained the skills necessary to package, scale, and manage your application efficiently.

With a focus on ensuring a secure and robust application, we discussed implementing **authentication and authorization** using **Spring Security** and **JWT.** These tools allow you to protect your application while providing a smooth login experience for your users. Moreover, you learned how to design and deploy **microservices** and even incorporate **serverless** components to achieve better scalability and fault isolation.

High availability and disaster recovery are crucial for keeping applications running smoothly despite hardware failures, high traffic, or unforeseen incidents. We covered advanced **high availability** strategies such as **multi-availability zones** and **load balancing,** and **disaster recovery** approaches like **warm standby** and **pilot light** configurations, giving you the knowledge needed to build resilient applications that ensure minimal downtime and fast recovery.

Real-time features have become a key requirement for many modern applications. We showed you how to use **WebSockets** and **STOMP** to add real-time capabilities like chat features or live notifications to your full stack application. Monitoring and logging were also highlighted as essential elements to maintain application health. By using **Prometheus, Grafana,** and **Elastic Stack (ELK),** you learned how to keep an eye on system performance, detect anomalies early, and troubleshoot effectively.

Ultimately, full stack development is not just about the technology stack; it's about building **real-world applications** that solve problems effectively, providing **seamless experiences** to users, and maintaining reliability in the face of unpredictable circumstances. By following the concepts, techniques, and practices discussed throughout this book, you have gained the skills to build, deploy, secure, and maintain sophisticated full stack applications that users can trust.

The path of a full stack developer is always evolving, with new tools, frameworks, and paradigms emerging constantly. Keep experimenting, keep learning, and most importantly, keep building. The skills and experiences you've gained in this journey lay a solid foundation, but it's up to you to continue growing and pushing the boundaries of what's possible in full stack development.

Thank you for embarking on this journey. May the skills you've learned here be the springboard for many successful projects to come!

www.ingramcontent.com/pod-product-compliance
Lightning Source LLC
La Vergne TN
LVHW051331050326
832903LV00031B/3469